CODE BREAKERS

Women Who Shaped the Digital World

By
Clara J. Sinclair

CODE BREAKERS

Women Who Shaped the Digital World

CONTENTS

INTRODUCTION

Technology, in its myriad forms, shapes our world every day. From the algorithms that curate our social media feeds to the software that controls spacecraft, the tech landscape is a complex, ever-evolving tapestry. Yet, for too long, the narratives of women pioneers who have played crucial roles in this digital revolution have been overshadowed or outright ignored. This book aims to rectify that by spotlighting the extraordinary women who have made significant contributions across various tech domains.

The road to progress in tech has been paved with the innovations, sacrifices, and resilience of countless individuals. Among these, the women featured in this book have made lasting impacts, often against significant odds. They have not only navigated but also excelled in a male-dominated field, driven by sheer brilliance, unyielding determination, and an unquenchable passion for discovery and improvement. Their stories are more than just historical footnotes; they are powerful testaments to what can be achieved when talent and opportunity intersect.

As we delve into these remarkable journeys, it's important to understand the societal challenges and professional hurdles these women faced. Imagine being one of the few women in a room filled with men, where your every idea is scrutinized more harshly, your every success diminished, and yet, rising above these biases with steadfast determination. These narratives aren't just about technical achievements; they're also about the human spirit transcending barriers. It's a story of grit, ingenuity, and ever-optimistic search for progress.

Whether it's Ada Lovelace, who envisioned the potential of computers long before they existed, or contemporary leaders like Kimberly Bryant, who is paving the way for the next generation of female coders, their individual stories form a collective narrative of innovation, perseverance, and change. They redefined what's possible, leading revolutions in their respective fields, from software engineering to artificial intelligence, from gaming to cybersecurity.

Understanding their contributions also helps us appreciate the broader context of technological evolution and, more importantly, the future. Each chapter of this book focuses on different aspects of tech, such as programming, hardware innovations, software trailblazing, and entrepreneurial ventures. By tracing these diverse pathways, we uncover not only the beat of the digital heart but also the human stories that give it rhythm. This exploration isn't just academic; it's deeply personal, aiming to inspire current and future generations of tech enthusiasts, especially women, to consider careers they may have deemed unreachable.

One can't underestimate the importance of representation. Seeing oneself in the stories of successful, trailblazing women transforms abstract dreams into attainable goals. For aspiring female engineers and tech professionals, these stories are not just motivation; they are blueprints for overcoming societal constraints and professional hurdles. Feminists and social change advocates will find in these pages powerful examples of progress toward gender equality and empowerment. Whether you are a seasoned professional or a young student just starting out, the experiences shared here will resonate with you and hopefully encourage you to forge your unique path in the tech world.

Equally crucial is recognizing that the journey of these women is far from over. The tech industry continues to evolve, and the need for diverse voices and perspectives becomes increasingly critical. The future lies in building inclusive technologies that cater to a diverse world, and who better to lead this charge than those who have already broken countless barriers to innovate and lead? Understanding their past contributions enables us to better shape a more inclusive and equitable future, where talent and hard work are the true measures of success, irrespective of gender.

Additionally, by chronicling these stories, we're actively participating in reshaping the narrative. This book contributes to a more accurate and inclusive history of technology that future generations will reference. It becomes part of a larger movement to recognize and celebrate contributions that have been marginalized or forgotten. As we honor these women, we don't just look back; we look forward with renewed hope and inspiration.

In essence, this book is a tribute to all women in tech — past, present, and future. It's a celebration of their achievements and a call to action for everyone to recognize and support the diverse talents that enrich the tech industry. Their stories remind us that technology is not just about code and circuits; it's about people, dreams, and the relentless pursuit of a better world. Through their eyes, we gain not only insights into technological advancements but also learn lessons in resilience, creativity, and the power of unwavering conviction.

So, as you flip through these pages, we hope you find more than just information. We aim to ignite a spark of curiosity, a desire for innovation, and an appreciation for the incredible women who have shaped, and are continuing to shape, the technological landscape. Let their stories inspire you to push boundaries, challenge norms, and contribute to the ever-evolving tapestry of technology with your unique voice and vision.

Welcome to a journey through time and innovation, where we unravel the threads of history to reveal the hidden figures behind the grand tapestry of technology. This is a tribute, an exploration, and a celebration of women in tech. Their legacy lives on in every line of code, every innovative solution, and every groundbreaking invention. It's time their stories were told, loud and clear, for the world to hear.

Chapter 1:
Pioneers of Programming

In a time when computers were the size of entire rooms and programming was a nascent field, the contributions of pioneering women in technology were nothing short of groundbreaking. The journey begins with Ada Lovelace, who envisioned the potential of computing machines long before code was even a concept. Then there's Grace Hopper, whose work laid the foundational stones of modern computing by developing the first compiler and advocating for machine-independent programming languages. Through their unwavering dedication, these trailblazers not only forged new realms of possibility but also broke societal expectations, setting the stage for the generations of women who would follow in their footsteps. Their stories are a testament to the incredible impact of visionaries who defied the norms and carved out a space for women in the tech world. This chapter dives into the lives of these extraordinary individuals, celebrating their achievements and illuminating their pivotal roles in the history of computing.

Ada Lovelace: The First Programmer

It's hard to imagine a time when the concept of programming didn't exist. Yet, during the early 19th century, one woman envisioned the capabilities of a machine long before computers became a reality. Her name was Ada Lovelace, and she's often celebrated as the world's first computer programmer. Ada's story is a testament to creativity, intellect, and the power of imagination, especially significant in a time when women were not expected to excel in the fields of science and mathematics.

Ada Lovelace was born in 1815 to Lord Byron, a famous poet, and Annabella Milbanke, a highly educated woman with a keen interest in mathematics. Ada's parents separated when she was very young, and her mother ensured that she received a rigorous education in math and science to counter what she saw as Lord Byron's dangerous poetic influence. This education laid the foundation for Ada's groundbreaking achievements in computer science.

Her intellectual pursuits led her to meet Charles Babbage, a mathematician and inventor who is credited with designing the first mechanical computer, known as the Analytical Engine. Babbage recognized Ada's exceptional analytical skills and intellect. They developed a significant professional relationship, with Ada translating a description of the Analytical Engine from Italian to English. However, her contribution didn't stop there; she added her own notes, which tripled the length of the original text. These notes are where Ada's genius truly shone.

In one of her most famous notes, Ada elaborated on how the Analytical Engine could be instructed to perform specified computations. This is where she conceptualized the idea of a "program." While Babbage had designed the machine, Ada understood its potential. She envisioned using it for purposes beyond numerical calculation—such as creating music or art. This was a radical idea at the time and positions Ada as a pioneer in the field of computational creativity.

It's not just what she envisioned but how she did it. Ada's approach to programming was multifaceted; she combined her analytical prowess with a poetic imagination that allowed her to see the broader implications of computational machinery. In her notes, she included what is often considered the first algorithm ever intended to be carried out by a machine. This recognition doesn't just make her the first programmer; it emphasizes the interdisciplinary nature of innovation.

Despite living in an era when women's intellectual contributions were often overshadowed, Ada's work did not go unnoticed. Her vision was both precise and profound. She understood that the Analytical Engine was not limited to arithmetic calculations but could be used to process symbols and create abstract, imaginative works. This broadened the scope of what machines could do and laid the groundwork for modern computing.

The importance of Ada's work cannot be overstated. Her contributions came to light only long after her death, as her notes resurfaced and were appreciated by later generations. Her ability to look beyond the immediate applications of a machine and see its potential for universal computation was revolutionary. Ada, in many ways, foresaw a digital world that would not materialize until over a century later.

Contemporary female engineers and programmers often look to Ada Lovelace as an inspirational figure. Her story is not just one of intellectual brilliance but also of perseverance and imagination. Ada's life challenges present-day women in tech to push beyond conventional boundaries and redefine what's possible. Today, her legacy is honored through numerous awards, events, and educational programs aimed at encouraging young women to pursue STEM fields.

Ada Lovelace Day is celebrated annually to honor her achievements and inspire future generations of women to pursue careers in science, technology, engineering, and mathematics (STEM). It's a day that underscores her enduring legacy and her role as a visionary who saw the poetic potential in numbers and machines.

The relevance of Ada's work extends far beyond her own lifetime. As we navigate an increasingly digital world, the principles she laid down continue to influence modern technology. From algorithms that power complex computations to the creative coding practices used in digital art and music, Ada's initial insights have become integral to our understanding of what machines can achieve.

Ada Lovelace's story serves as a beacon of inspiration for aspiring female engineers, tech enthusiasts, and anyone with a passion for the intersection of creativity and technology. Her ability to transcend the limitations of her time and envision a future rich with possibilities remains a crucial lesson for innovators today.

Grace Hopper: The Queen of Code

Grace Hopper was a force of nature in the world of computing, a titan who defied boundaries and broke barriers with her keen intellect and relentless drive. Born in 1906, Hopper's fascination with machines began at a young age. Known as "Amazing Grace" to colleagues and admirers, she had a pioneering spirit that led her to become one of the most influential figures in the realm of computer science. Her journey was not just about technical achievements but also about inspiring generations of future engineers and programmers.

Hopper's academic journey started at Vassar College, where she graduated with a degree in mathematics and physics. She then earned her master's degree and Ph.D. in mathematics from Yale University, an impressive feat for a woman in the 1930s. Her deep understanding of mathematics was the foundation upon which she built her groundbreaking work in computer science. But Hopper's contributions weren't confined to academia; she had a vision of making computers accessible and comprehensible to a wider audience.

When World War II erupted, Hopper took an unexpected turn in her career. She joined the United States Navy, where her mathematical expertise was put to use in the war effort. It was within the Navy that she became one of the first programmers of the Harvard Mark I computer, one of the earliest electro-mechanical computers. The Mark I was a behemoth, stretching 51 feet long and weighing nearly five tons. It was an intimidating machine, yet Hopper was undeterred, immersing herself in the intricacies of computer programming.

One of Hopper's most celebrated contributions to computer science was her work on the development of COBOL (Common Business-Oriented Language). Prior to COBOL, programming languages were highly specialized and required intimate knowledge of the machine's hardware. Hopper envisioned a more human-readable language that could simplify programming tasks for businesses and government agencies. COBOL has since become one of the most enduring programming languages, underscoring her forward-thinking approach.

Her innovative work didn't stop there. Hopper believed that computers should serve humans, not the other way around. To that end, she developed the first compiler, a system that translates human-readable code into machine code. This revolutionary concept laid the groundwork for modern programming languages and opened up the field to people who may not have had a deep understanding of computer hardware. Her compiler, known as the A-0 System, was a monumental step forward, setting the stage for future advancements in software development.

Hopper's ability to bridge the gap between machine language and human language was pioneering. She envisioned a future where computing would be more intuitive and user-friendly. Her work directly contributed to the democratization of computer science, making it more accessible to a broader audience. This was a significant shift from the arcane and highly specialized world of early computing, and it's a testament to her innovative spirit.

Moreover, Grace Hopper was an advocate for education and a mentor to many budding computer scientists. She frequently gave lectures and speeches, often emphasizing the need to embrace new technology and methodologies. Hopper famously said, "The most damaging phrase in the language is 'We've always done it this way.'" Her words resonate deeply even today, emphasizing the importance of innovation and questioning the status quo.

While her technical contributions were monumental, Hopper's influence extended far beyond her inventions. She became a symbol of what women could achieve in a male-dominated field. Her work and her career were trailblazing, serving as an inspiration for countless women who followed. She demonstrated that gender should never be a barrier to achieving greatness in science and technology. Her achievements were a clarion call to young women everywhere that their aspirations were valid and attainable.

In her later years, Hopper continued to receive accolades for her contributions to the field of computer science. She was awarded the National Medal of Technology in 1991 and posthumously received the Presidential Medal of Freedom in 2016. These honors were a recognition not just of her technical achievements but also of her role as a pioneer who broke down barriers and paved the way for future generations.

Her legacy lives on in many ways. The "Grace Hopper Celebration of Women in Computing" is an annual conference that brings together thousands of women in technology to celebrate their contributions and inspire future leaders. This event embodies Hopper's spirit of innovation, education, and empowerment, continuing her mission to make the tech world more inclusive and accessible.

Indeed, Grace Hopper's story is one of resilience, innovation, and relentless pursuit of knowledge. Her life's work laid the foundation for modern computing and demonstrated the transformative power of technology. She championed the idea that computing should be accessible to all and not just the domain of a few specialists. This idea has had a lasting impact on the field and continues to shape the future of technology.

For tech enthusiasts, aspiring female engineers, and anyone interested in the inspirational stories of real-life heroes, Grace Hopper's life offers a profound lesson. Her journey illustrates that with passion, perseverance, and a willingness to defy norms, one can achieve remarkable things. Hopper's legacy is a testament to the power of innovation and the importance of making technology accessible and inclusive for everyone.

In closing, Grace Hopper was not just the "Queen of Code" but a visionary who saw the potential for computing to transform the world. Her work and her spirit continue to inspire and challenge us to think bigger, push boundaries, and never stop questioning. She was a true pioneer of programming and a beacon of possibility for all who follow in her footsteps.

Chapter 2:
Breaking Barriers

Breaking Barriers isn't just a phrase; it's a testament to resilience and fortitude echoing through the annals of tech history. Our journey unfolds with the inspiring tales of the ENIAC Six, who defied societal norms to become the unsung heroes of the early digital age, and Evelyn Boyd Granville, a mathematician whose brilliance illuminated the shadows cast by racial and gender prejudices. These pioneering women didn't just carve paths for themselves but blazed trails for countless others, demonstrating that determination and skill know no boundaries. Traversing through hostile terrains, they shattered glass ceilings and opened doors wide for future generations of women in technology. Their stories underscore a crucial lesson: barriers are meant to be broken, and in their breaking, new worlds of opportunities emerge.

The ENIAC Six: Unsung Heroes of the Early Digital Age

The story of the ENIAC Six is one of determination, ingenuity, and breaking barriers in a male-dominated industry. During World War II, the U.S. Army needed a way to calculate artillery trajectories efficiently. The answer was the Electronic Numerical Integrator and Computer (ENIAC), the first general-purpose digital computer. Yet, while the male engineers who designed the hardware were lauded, the women who programmed it were largely overlooked. These six remarkable women—Frances Bilas, Jean Jennings, Betty Snyder, Marlyn Wescoff,

Kathleen McNulty, and Ruth Lichterman—deserve to be remembered as pioneers in programming.

As the ENIAC was being developed, these women, many of whom had degrees in mathematics, were recruited to solve complex equations by hand. They acquiesced to the challenge, unaware that they would soon transition from human "computers" to programmers of a groundbreaking machine. Their work required not just mathematical understanding but also immense creativity and logical reasoning. As they worked with the ENIAC, they wrote the machine's first set of instructions, laying the groundwork for future programming languages.

The conditions under which they worked were anything but ideal. The ENIAC's environment was purely experimental, replete with trial and error. There were no manuals, no existing literature, and certainly no mentors in the field of programming to guide them. They relied on their intellectual prowess and synergistic teamwork to develop methods for coding the machine. The task was daunting, the pressure immense, but these women exhibited an extraordinary level of resilience. They were not just following instructions—they were creating them.

Each of these women brought unique skills and perspectives to the project. For instance, Kathleen McNulty, born to Irish immigrants and deeply invested in mathematics, used her talents to enhance the computational capabilities of the ENIAC. Jean Jennings, another diligent mathematician, understood the importance of optimizing the computer's use, which involved analyzing and redesigning processes to improve efficiency. These were no small feats. Each stroke of their pen, each punch in a card, represented a step forward in a previously uncharted realm of technological capability.

Their contributions were critical during the war, but the importance of their work extended far beyond that turbulent period. The methodologies they crafted under necessity evolved into the principles on which modern computing rests. They essentially invented primitive versions of debugging and optimization—concepts now fundamental to software development. While their male counterparts were celebrated publicly, the ENIAC Six worked away from the spotlight, largely unrecognized for their creative genius.

Recognition is critical, not only for honoring these pioneers but also for inspiring future generations. The challenges they overcame resonate deeply with issues faced by women in technology today. Despite being in an era where female contributions were often overshadowed, these women stood out by their competence and determination. They broke barriers not only in the technical complexities they mastered but also in the societal expectations they defied.

The cultural conditions of the 1940s and 1950s were rigid and unforgiving when it came to gender roles. Women were expected to fulfill domestic duties, and careers in science and technology were considered unfit. Yet, the ENIAC Six shunned these stereotypes, driven by their passion for mathematics and the unique opportunity to engage in groundbreaking work. In a way, their journey mirrors the larger societal shifts toward gender equality that were beginning to take place.

It's important to consider the impact of their work in the broader context of women in STEM fields. They serve as a testament to the fact that talent and ingenuity know no gender. By excelling in a male-dominated field with little to no guidance, they set a precedent for what women could achieve in technology. Their story is not just one of historical significance but of ongoing relevance. It highlights the importance of perseverance, collaboration, and the courage to defy societal norms.

Betty Snyder, who later became known as Betty Holberton, continued to contribute significantly to the field of computing beyond her work on the ENIAC. She was instrumental in developing early programming languages like COBOL and FORTRAN, which revolutionized business and scientific computing. Her tireless efforts exemplify how the experiences and skills gained from working on the ENIAC served as a launching pad for further innovation.

Similarly, Jean Jennings, who became Jean Jennings Bartik, also made substantial contributions post-ENIAC. Her work on BINAC and UNIVAC continued to push the frontiers of what was possible in computing. These early machines were the predecessors of the computers that would later revolutionize industries and personal life. The foundations laid by the ENIAC Six's programming not only facilitated the success of these machines but also helped shape the future of digital computing.

Marlyn Wescoff and Frances Bilas (who became Fran Bilas Spence and Marlyn Wescoff Melvin, respectively) moved on to other roles but remained influential in the tech community by sharing their experiences, thus inspiring new generations. Ruth Lichterman (later Ruth Lichterman Teitelbaum) continued her contributions in computer mathematics and education, highlighting the lasting impact of their pioneering efforts.

When people reflect on the history of computing, the importance of the ENIAC Six should be front and center. Their story is not just about six women who contributed to a wartime effort. It's about the limitless potential of intellectual curiosity and the power of breaking barriers. Today's tech environment, with its emphasis on diversity and inclusion, owes a debt to these early trailblazers.

In retrospect, the achievements of the ENIAC Six are magnified by the adversities they faced. Operating in a nascent field with no clear guidelines, they paved the way through sheer perseverance and ingenuity. Their legacy is a profound reminder that behind every major technological advancement, there are often unsung heroes whose stories need to be told. The narrative of the ENIAC Six challenges us to recognize and celebrate the diverse voices that have shaped technology.

Understanding their journey enriches our appreciation for the complexities of early programming and provides a valuable lesson in resilience and teamwork. It underscores the notion that breaking barriers involves not just technological advances but also the courage to defy social norms. The spirit of the ENIAC Six lives on in every woman who has courageously pursued a career in tech, proving that the seeds of change planted decades ago continue to flourish.

In closing, the contributions of the ENIAC Six are far greater than the roles they were initially given. Their work has had ripple effects that are still felt today, setting the stage for future generations of women in computing. And as we consider the future of technology, it's vital to remember and honor those who laid the foundations, often in the shadows, allowing us to see more clearly the path ahead.

Evelyn Boyd Granville: Overcoming Racial and Gender Hurdles

When you think about pioneers in mathematics and computer science, the name Evelyn Boyd Granville might not come to mind immediately. But it should. Granville represents a unique and powerful story of persistence, ingenuity, and breaking barriers that seemed insurmountable to most. Born in 1924 in Washington, D.C., Evelyn Boyd Granville grew up during the Great Depression, a time when opportunities for African Americans, particularly women, were scarce. Her journey from a young girl fascinated by numbers to becoming one of the first African American women to earn a Ph.D. in mathematics is a narrative of resilience and groundbreaking achievements.

Granville's early life was shaped by the support of her mother and her teachers, who encouraged her academic pursuits despite the racial and gender biases of the era. Her mother, Julia Walker Boyd, worked tirelessly to provide for Evelyn and her sister, understanding the importance of education in a world that often denied such opportunities to Black families. Granville recognized early on that education was her path to freedom and empowerment, a mantra she carried throughout her career.

Her academic prowess was evident from the get-go. She excelled in school and was awarded a scholarship to attend Smith College, a predominantly white institution. At Smith, Granville encountered a different set of challenges—racism and sexism were persistent, often manifesting in subtle yet debilitating ways. However, these obstacles only fueled her determination. With unwavering focus, she graduated summa cum laude and received several honors, including election to Phi Beta Kappa, the prestigious honor society.

Granville's academic journey didn't stop with her undergraduate degree. She went on to earn a master's degree and a Ph.D. from Yale University, making her one of the first African American women to achieve such a feat in mathematics. Surpassing these milestone achievements wasn't just a personal victory; it was a historic moment that changed the landscape for future generations of women and minorities in STEM fields.

Despite her qualifications, Granville faced a challenging job market filled with discrimination. Working initially as an instructor at various institutions, she found it difficult to secure a tenure-track position. This led her to take on roles at government agencies, where she ultimately made significant contributions. At IBM, she worked on the Project Mercury space program, developing computer software that laid the groundwork for America's manned space missions.

IBM wasn't just a stepping stone but a place where Granville could showcase her brilliance in problem-solving and analytical thinking. She excelled in creating algorithms and writing programs that were instrumental in the success of these early space missions. Her work wasn't just technical but transformational, demonstrating the critical role that African American women could play in science and technology.

Her contributions weren't limited to her technical achievements. Granville was also an advocate for education and spent a significant part of her career teaching. She taught at Fisk University, where she once was a student, and later at California State University. In these roles, she aimed to inspire and educate the next generation of mathematicians and computer scientists, particularly those from underrepresented groups.

Granville's story is a vivid testament to the idea that breaking barriers isn't just about individual accolades; it's about creating pathways for others to follow. Her commitment to education extended beyond the classroom as she participated in programs designed to encourage women and minorities to pursue STEM careers. She believed that true progress in science and technology would only be achieved through diversity and inclusion.

It's easy to talk about diversity and inclusion today as buzzwords, but Granville lived these principles long before they became popular. Her life's work broke stereotypes and challenged the societal norms that kept many out of the scientific community. Granville's ability to thrive in an environment that was often unwelcoming speaks volumes about her character and resolve.

Furthermore, Granville's story isn't just about overcoming obstacles; it's about what can be accomplished when those barriers are removed. Her innovations are woven into the fabric of modern computer science and mathematics, demonstrating the untold potential that lay dormant in those sidelined by prejudice and discrimination.

In recognizing Evelyn Boyd Granville, we celebrate more than just a mathematician; we honor a trailblazer whose life and work continue to inspire. Her legacy is a call to arms for anyone who faces barriers due to race, gender, or any other societal impositions—it's a reminder that determination, skill, and support can help one rise above seemingly insurmountable hurdles.

Granville's journey through academia, industry, and education serves as an enduring symbol of progress and possibility. Her story is not just one for the history books but a vibrant, living narrative that continues to inspire tech enthusiasts, aspiring female engineers, feminists, and those who crave stories of real-life heroism against all odds. Evelyn Boyd Granville didn't just overcome the racial and gender-based hurdles placed in her path; she shattered them and paved the way for future pioneers.

As we look to the future, let us draw lessons from her remarkable journey: the value of persistence, the importance of a supportive community, and the impact one individual can make when they strive to change the status quo. The achievements of Evelyn Boyd Granville remind us that while barriers may exist, they are not insurmountable. And in overcoming them, we not only uplift ourselves but also create a better, more inclusive world for all.

CHAPTER 3:
REVOLUTIONIZING THE INDUSTRY

In a world dominated by stark technological challenges and gender imbalances, Mary Allen Wilkes and Dorothy Vaughan emerge as guiding lights, transforming the industry through innovative vision and determined leadership. Mary Allen Wilkes, often remembered as the early face of user experience, broke new ground with her exceptional work on the LINC computer, putting user-centric design at the heart of computing. Dorothy Vaughan, a formidable force at NASA, not merely led hidden figures but also laid down the groundwork for future generations to breach the walls of racial and gender discrimination. These women didn't just participate in the industry; they revolutionized it, proving that persistence and brilliance know no bounds. While their journeys are testament to the power of breaking molds and reimagining possibilities, they also serve as inspirational sagas, epitomizing how courage and intellect can fundamentally reshape the technological landscape.

Mary Allen Wilkes: The Early Face of User Experience

Mary Allen Wilkes is a name that often doesn't get the limelight it deserves, overshadowed by more prominent figures in the tech industry. However, her contributions were nothing short of groundbreaking and have set the stage for what we now call user experience (UX).

Born in 1937, Mary Allen Wilkes was a visionary who saw the potential of computers long before they were a staple in our daily lives.

She pioneered a way of thinking about computers that would make them accessible and practical for everyday people, not just the tech-savvy or scientific community. This foresight is what makes her one of the early faces of user experience, a field that would transform the way humans interact with machines.

Wilkes was part of a transformative era when computers were enormous machines filling entire rooms and operated primarily by specialized technicians. Early computers were anything but user-friendly. These daunting, massive machines were far from the personal computers we use today. Navigating these systems required not just intelligence but also the kind of persistence and vision that Mary Allen Wilkes possessed in abundance.

Her journey began at the Lincoln Laboratory at the Massachusetts Institute of Technology (MIT), where she initially joined as a programmer. It was here that she would work on the LINC (Laboratory INstrument Computer) project, a groundbreaking endeavor aimed at creating a more interactive and user-friendly computing experience. The LINC, one of the first personal computers, was designed to assist biomedical researchers in their tasks, making complex computations more accessible.

The significance of the LINC project can't be overstated. The LINC was an early forerunner to the personal computer and played a crucial role in transitioning from the era of room-sized machines to compact, user-focused devices. Mary Allen Wilkes was at the heart of this paradigm shift. She designed the operating system for the LINC, creating tools and interfaces that allowed scientists to interact with the computer in real-time. This was a monumental leap forward in making computers more accessible to everyday users.

It's worth noting that creating software in the 1960s was vastly different compared to today's standards. There were no libraries of pre-written code or sophisticated development environments. Programmers like Wilkes had to start from scratch, writing their programs directly in machine language. This required an intimate understanding of both hardware and software, and even then, debugging was an immensely tedious process. Wilkes tackled these challenges head-on, demonstrating an exceptional ability to bridge the gap between complex computational theory and practical user needs.

Beyond her technical prowess, Mary Allen Wilkes brought an empathetic understanding of user needs to her work. She knew that for computers to become essential tools in various fields, they had to be designed with the user in mind. This might sound obvious today, but at the time, it was a revolutionary concept. She strived to create systems that were intuitive and lowered the barrier to entry for people who were not computer scientists. This empathetic approach laid the groundwork for modern UX design principles, which prioritize the user's experience above all else.

One of the most iconic stories showcasing Wilkes' innovative spirit and dedication involves her setting up the LINC computer in her home. In 1965, it was almost unthinkable for a computer to exist outside of a laboratory or corporate setting. Undeterred by the norms of her time, Wilkes became the first person to use a personal computer in a home environment. This was not just a technical achievement but a symbolic act that foreshadowed the eventual democratization of computing technology. She proved that computers could be integrated into personal spaces, further advancing the case for user-friendly design.

Mary Allen Wilkes' work on the LINC and her advocacy for user-centric design left an indelible mark on the computing industry. Her contributions were foundational to the development of personal computers and have influenced generations of UX designers, software engineers, and tech enthusiasts. She showed that empathy and technical expertise could coexist, and indeed must coexist, to create truly revolutionary technology.

She not only broke ground in the technical aspects of computing but also demonstrated resilience and an unyielding commitment to progress at a time when women were grossly underrepresented in the field of technology. Her story is inspirational for aspiring female engineers and feminists alike, showing that barriers, no matter how formidable, can be overcome with talent, tenacity, and a vision for a better future.

Today, when we interact with our smartphones, use apps with seamless interfaces, or perform complex tasks without needing a computer science degree, we are standing on the shoulders of giants like Mary Allen Wilkes. Her early work in making computers user-friendly laid the roadmap for what would become a multi-billion-dollar industry centered around enhancing user experience. She wasn't just programming a computer; she was programming the future of how humans would interact with machines.

In an industry that is continually evolving, where new technologies emerge at a breakneck pace, Wilkes' approach to user-centric design remains as relevant as ever. Her story serves as a powerful reminder that the most impactful technological advancements often arise from a simple yet profound question: What's best for the user? This focus on usability and accessibility is now a cornerstone of product design, software development, and human-computer interaction.

In acknowledging her contributions, we not only honor Mary Allen Wilkes but also inspire new generations of tech enthusiasts to think big and stay committed to user-centric innovation. Her legacy is a testament to what can be achieved when talent meets opportunity, guided by a vision that puts people at the heart of technology.

The journey of Mary Allen Wilkes is more than a chapter in the history of computing; it is a beacon for what is possible when you dare to defy norms and envision a future where technology serves all. Her work continues to influence the industry, reminding us that the early face of user experience was shaped by a pioneer who saw the potential for computers to be not just powerful, but also accessible and indispensable tools in our everyday lives.

Dorothy Vaughan: Leading Hidden Figures

Dorothy Vaughan's name might not be the first that comes to mind when we think of groundbreaking figures in the tech world, but her contributions are nothing short of revolutionary. In an era characterized by segregation and limited opportunities for women, especially African-American women, Vaughan not only carved out a place for herself but also paved the way for future generations.

Dorothy was a gifted mathematician and an exceptional leader. Born in 1910, she grew up during a time when racial and gender barriers were deeply entrenched in American society. Despite these obstacles, she graduated from Wilberforce University, a historically black college, with a degree in mathematics. Her passion for mathematics and determination to succeed despite societal limitations set the stage for her trailblazing career.

In 1943, Vaughan joined the National Advisory Committee for Aeronautics (NACA), the precursor to NASA, as a member of the segregated computing unit known as the West Area Computing Unit. This group was composed of African-American female mathematicians who manually performed complex calculations. Despite the unit's crucial work, its members were often overlooked and underrated, confined to segregated offices with separate dining and restroom facilities.

Vaughan's ability to lead shone brightly early in her career. When the West Area Computing Unit's head unexpectedly left, Vaughan stepped up, becoming not only the acting head but also the first African-American supervisor at NACA. Her leadership went beyond producing accurate and timely calculations; she was a mentor and an advocate for her team. She ensured that the women working under her got the recognition they deserved and had opportunities to advance their careers.

The advent of electronic computers in the 1960s transformed the world of computation, and Vaughan foresaw this change. Recognizing that programming skills would be crucial, she learned FORTRAN, one of the earliest high-level programming languages, and encouraged her team to do the same. This proactive adaptation ensured that she and her team remained indispensable as the organization transitioned from manual to electronic calculations. Vaughan's ability to anticipate industry shifts and respond with agility is a lesson in resilience and foresight.

It's impossible to tell Vaughan's story without also acknowledging the broader impact she had on the space race. Her work directly contributed to significant milestones, including the launch of astronaut John Glenn into orbit. As depicted in the book and subsequent film "Hidden Figures," Vaughan, along with colleagues Mary Jackson and Katherine Johnson, played a pivotal role in ensuring the accuracy of Glenn's orbital flight calculations. Their contributions were critical not only to the success of the mission but also to the safety of the astronauts.

Moreover, Vaughan's legacy is a testament to the power of collective effort. She believed in collaboration and understood that rising tides lift all boats. Her emphasis on teamwork, mutual support, and shared knowledge cultivated an environment where each woman's strengths were amplified, creating a powerful unit capable of overcoming immense challenges. This collective spirit is a cornerstone of modern project management and organizational behavior practices.

Dorothy Vaughan retired from NASA in 1971, but her influence did not wane. The pathways she forged created more inclusive spaces for women and people of color in STEM fields. Her story serves as an enduring inspiration, demonstrating that change often starts with one person willing to challenge the status quo and lift others along the way.

Vaughan's journey from a segregated computing office to the forefront of the space race exemplifies a profound narrative of courage and resilience. She not only excelled in a highly technical field but did so in an environment that often tried to diminish her contributions. Her leadership went beyond her analytical skills; it was her ability to mentor, advocate, and envision a future where her team's potential was fully realized that truly set her apart.

Her story inspires today's tech enthusiasts and industry leaders to seek out and cultivate diverse talent. In a world still grappling with issues of representation and equity, Vaughan's life is a powerful reminder that excellence knows no color or gender. It encourages aspiring female engineers and technologists to pursue their ambitions relentlessly and to support others on their journey.

In reflecting upon Vaughan's legacy, it's crucial to also acknowledge the numerous unnamed and unseen heroes who, like her, made monumental contributions to the fields of mathematics, science, and technology. These hidden figures changed the world, often without the recognition they deserved, and their collective accomplishments remind us of the importance of inclusivity in innovation.

The narrative of Dorothy Vaughan is as much about individual brilliance as it is about the transformation of an industry. Her work helped NASA transition into a new era of space exploration, underscoring the fundamental truth that diversity and inclusion are not merely ethical imperatives but keys to unlocking potential and driving revolutionary advancements. This legacy of impact and inspiration continues to motivate and guide us as we venture into future frontiers of technology and exploration.

CHAPTER 4:
INNOVATORS IN HARDWARE

In the intricate world of hardware engineering, Frances Allen and Lynn Conway stand out as trailblazing innovators who've reshaped the landscape of computational technology. Frances Allen, known for her groundbreaking work in compiler optimization, brought software and hardware closer by making programs run more efficiently. Her contributions were pivotal in transforming how computers process information, marking a significant leap in system performance. On the other hand, Lynn Conway revolutionized microchip design with her pioneering techniques in VLSI (Very Large Scale Integration). Her work not only made microchips more powerful and compact but also democratized chip design, opening doors for countless engineers and startups. Together, Allen and Conway exemplify the power of innovation in hardware, proving that visionary thinking and relentless dedication can drive transformative change in technology.

Frances Allen: Compiler Pioneer

In the realm of computing, Frances Allen's contributions stand as towering milestones, pushing the boundaries of what computers could achieve. Her groundbreaking work on compilers—programs that translate high-level code into machine language—didn't just enhance the efficiency of computing processes. It deeply influenced the architecture of hardware systems as well. Allen consistently broke down barriers in a male-dominated field, emerging as a luminary whose visionary insights continue to impact technology today.

Born in Peru, New York, in 1932, Frances Allen grew up with a passion for mathematics and teaching. Initially setting out to be a schoolteacher, she earned a degree in mathematics from The Teachers College at SUNY Albany. However, her career took a dramatic turn when she joined IBM in 1957 with the initial intention of saving money to pay off her student loans. Little did she know that this decision would lead her to become one of the most influential figures in computer science.

Allen's initial work at IBM involved teaching new employees about Fortran—the first high-level programming language developed by John Backus and his team. However, she soon moved on to more technical challenges. One of her first major projects was working on the Stretch-Harvest project, a high-level effort involving supercomputers designed for the National Security Agency. Allen's expertise in optimization led her to focus on compilers, specifically how they could be improved to make programs run faster and more efficiently.

While working on Stretch-Harvest, Allen developed a series of groundbreaking techniques for optimizing compilers. Her innovative use of flow analysis for automatic code optimization allowed programs to be more efficient, effectively transforming raw computing power into practical, usable performance. These techniques became the cornerstone for modern compiler design.

The significance of Allen's work on compilers can't be overstated. By improving the efficiency of these translating programs, she enabled software to run more quickly and use less memory. This had a profound impact on the development of hardware, as more efficient software translated into less demanding requirements for processing power and memory capacity. In this way, Allen's work effectively bridged the gap between software and hardware, making them evolve hand in hand toward greater efficiency and capability.

In addition to her technical achievements, Frances Allen also broke down significant gender barriers in her field. In 1989, she became the first woman to be named an IBM Fellow, a prestigious recognition of her groundbreaking work and contributions to the field. This honor was not just a personal achievement but also served as an inspiration for countless other women in technology. Allen showed that with passion, dedication, and talent, it was possible to surmount the gender biases that had long plagued the technology industry.

Her influence extended beyond her direct contributions to compiler technology and hardware optimization. Allen was a dedicated mentor and advocate for women in computing. She played an instrumental role in the development of IBM's diversity initiatives, nurturing future generations of female engineers and technologists. By sharing her knowledge and experiences, she provided a path for other women to follow, helping them to overcome the barriers she herself had faced.

One of the remarkable aspects of Allen's career is how her early contributions continue to resonate in the field of computing. Even as technology has evolved rapidly, the foundational principles she established remain relevant. Advanced modern compilers still use many of the optimization techniques she developed, and her work continues to be a touchstone for new researchers and engineers looking to push the boundaries of computing.

Into her later years, Frances Allen remained a prolific and passionate advocate for the importance of women in technology. She continually emphasized the need for diversity and inclusivity, understanding that varied perspectives were crucial for innovation. She participated actively in numerous initiatives aimed at encouraging young women to pursue careers in science, technology, engineering, and math (STEM). Her life's work went beyond her own achievements to uplift others who might follow in her footsteps.

Frances Allen retired from IBM in 2002 but continued to stay engaged with the technology community. Her lasting impact on both hardware and software development is undeniable, as her pioneering work on compiler optimization continues to underpin much of modern computing. Moreover, her story stands as a testament to what can be achieved when talent meets opportunity and determination.

A genuine visionary, Allen's career serves as a beacon for aspiring technologists of all genders. She broke through glass ceilings and shattered stereotypes, showing that women could not only participate in but also lead the advance of technology. Her legacy is not just in the code that runs quietly behind the scenes of our digital world but also in the lives she touched and the paths she cleared for future generations.

Allen once stated, "It's an exciting time to be a part of the evolution of computing technology. We have only begun to scratch the surface of what is possible." Her words remain prophetic. As new technologies like artificial intelligence, quantum computing, and advanced machine learning emerge, they stand on the shoulders of giants like Frances Allen. She laid the groundwork that continues to enable profound advancements, proving that the sky is not the limit; rather, it is just the beginning.

Lynn Conway: Innovating Microchip Design

At a time when the concept of a "microchip" was in its nascent stages, Lynn Conway emerged as a transformative force whose insights would ultimately shape the very architecture of modern computing. A pioneering figure in her field, Conway became an unsung hero whose groundbreaking innovations and personal resilience serve as an enduring source of inspiration. Her work not only revolutionized microchip design but also set an example of courage and authenticity in the face of adversity.

Born in 1938, Conway's early years were marked by a burning curiosity for how things worked. Her affinity for mathematics and science could be traced back to her childhood, where she showed promise far beyond her years. Despite facing numerous challenges from her environment and society, Conway's tenacity ensured she pursued her passion. Graduating from MIT in 1962 with a degree in electrical engineering, she went on to join IBM, an environment rife with possibility yet undoubtedly challenging for women engineers.

Her work at IBM centered around the architecture of the Stretch project, one of the earliest efforts in supercomputing. However, Conway's trajectory took a dramatic turn when she was fired from IBM after disclosing her intention to transition genders. This monumental personal challenge could have halted her career entirely, yet it became a powerful turning point. Through courage and unyielding resolve, Conway re-entered the field, ultimately securing a role at the famed Xerox Palo Alto Research Center (PARC).

At PARC, Conway found herself surrounded by visionaries and a culture that nurtured innovation. It was here that she teamed up with Carver Mead to develop VLSI (Very Large Scale Integration) design methodology. Their collaboration was not just a technical accomplishment but a revolutionary shift that democratized microchip design. This VLSI system essentially decomposed the complex process of chip design into more manageable segments, making it accessible to a broader range of engineers and designers.

The publication of their groundbreaking book, "Introduction to VLSI Systems," co-authored with Carver Mead in 1980, served as a pivotal moment for the electronics industry. This textbook became an essential resource, introducing new principles and standards for chip design that stand to this day. The VLSI design methodology allowed engineers to use computer-aided design (CAD) tools, revolutionizing the speed and efficiency of creating and testing new chip architectures.

This shift enabled the rapid advancement of microprocessors, making modern computing devices cheaper, more powerful, and more accessible.

Lynn Conway's contributions extended beyond her written work. In the early '80s, she organized the Multi-University Research Initiative, fostering collaboration across disciplines and institutions. She also spearheaded the "VLSI Design Courses" that democratized advanced technological education by promoting hands-on experience in microchip design for students and professionals alike. These courses became the breeding ground for the next generation of tech innovators who would drive forward the rapid advancements in electronics and computing.

But Conway's journey was not limited to technical advancements. Her personal story is a beacon of resilience and authenticity. Returning to academia as a professor at the University of Michigan in the late '80s and early '90s, she openly shared her journey of transformation. This transparency fostered an inclusive environment in a field historically dominated by men, encouraging future engineers and technologists to pursue their passions regardless of societal constraints.

Understanding Conway's impact also involves recognizing her as a role model for aspiring female engineers, and indeed, anyone who faces societal barriers. Her work illuminated a path not just for technological innovators but also for those seeking to live authentically in their personal and professional lives. Conway's legacy serves as a powerful reminder of the extraordinary outcomes that can arise when one's identity is embraced rather than hidden.

In an era where inclusion remains a critical issue in tech, Conway's advocacy for diversity cannot be overstated. She actively engaged in promoting STEM education for women and underrepresented groups, providing mentorship and serving as an inspiration for numerous individuals who would go on to make their own mark in the tech landscape. Her advocacy exemplifies the belief that innovation thrives in diverse and inclusive environments.

Lynn Conway: Innovating Microchip Design remains a key chapter in the history of technology, highlighting not just the technical advancements she spearheaded but also the profound human elements of perseverance, innovation, and authenticity. Her journey tells us that true innovation often comes from individuals who dare to challenge the status quo, those who are willing to confront and overcome personal and societal barriers.

In reflecting on Conway's journey, it's clear that her legacy continues to inspire and empower. Whether through the revolutionary VLSI design principles or her advocacy for an inclusive environment, Lynn Conway's story is a testament to the power of resilience and the transformative impact of inclusivity in driving forward innovation.

Chapter 5:
Software Trailblazers

In a world dominated by algorithms and code, the contributions of female software trailblazers like Barbara Liskov and Radia Perlman have paved the way for modern computing. Liskov, a titan of programming languages, laid the foundation for object-oriented programming, influencing countless software systems we rely on today. On the other hand, Perlman's innovations in network protocols are the backbone of the internet, earning her the title "Mother of the Internet." These women not only broke new ground in their respective fields but also shattered the glass ceiling, inspiring future generations to believe in the power of persistence and ingenuity. Their stories resonate deeply, urging us to recognize and celebrate the champions who help bridge the gender gap in technology, embodying the relentless spirit that drives the digital age forward.

Barbara Liskov: Foundations of Programming Languages

Barbara Liskov's contributions to computer science constitute some of the most critical groundwork in the field of programming languages. Her story is not just one of academic success but one of vision, resilience, and unrelenting curiosity. Born Barbara Jane Huberman in 1939, her journey from a young girl fascinated by numbers to an acclaimed computer scientist is a tale that embodies the transformative power of education and determination.

Growing up in California, she immersed herself in mathematics and science, fields that few women then explored. She graduated from the University of California, Berkeley, with a degree in mathematics. The era was thick with gender bias and societal norms that often relegated women to roles far removed from scientific inquiry. However, Liskov was not one to be deterred by societal expectations.

Her foray into computer science came at a time when the field was still in its nascent stages. She was one of the first women to earn a Ph.D. in computer science in the United States from Stanford University in 1968. Attaining her doctorate was an achievement unto itself, but it was only the beginning of a career that would profoundly impact software engineering and programming language design.

An influential part of Liskov's legacy is the Liskov Substitution Principle, a fundamental concept in object-oriented programming. This principle stipulates that objects of a superclass should be replaceable with objects of a subclass without altering the correctness of the program. Liskov's work in this area has provided developers with a conceptual framework that enhances code robustness and maintainability, making complex software systems more reliable and easier to manage.

Essentially, Liskov's research helped lay the groundwork for many of the object-oriented programming languages we rely on today, such as C++, Java, and Python. Her pioneering efforts did not stop at theoretical contributions. Practical implementations of her ideas have revolutionized how software applications are built, making her influence pervasive in the world of computing.

One of the crowning achievements of Liskov's career is the development of the CLU programming language. Created in the mid-1970s, CLU introduced several new concepts and data types that were groundbreaking at the time. It contributed to the evolution of modern programming languages by introducing data abstraction, a concept that allows data to be manipulated without needing to consider its implementation. This innovation is at the heart of contemporary software design, enabling developers to build more complex, efficient, and reusable software components.

Through CLU, Liskov demonstrated not just the power of abstraction but also the importance of modularity in software engineering. Her work encouraged a more disciplined approach to software development, wherein code could be divided into smaller, manageable pieces. This modular approach alleviated the burden of understanding and maintaining vast codebases, setting the stage for the development practices used today.

Beyond her technical contributions, Liskov has also been a profound advocate for women in STEM. Her career is a testament to breaking barriers and challenging the notion that certain fields are not 'suitable' for women. She has been a mentor and inspiration to countless female engineers, urging them to pursue their interests fearlessly and persistently.

In 2008, Liskov's humbling and impressive accomplishments were recognized with the Turing Award, often regarded as the Nobel Prize of computing. The award was a nod not just to her innovations but to the enduring impact of her work on the entire field of computer science. Her acceptance speech emphasized the importance of curiosity and lifelong learning, virtues that have clearly guided her through decades of groundbreaking work.

Her admirable journey highlights an essential lesson: the field of computer science, like many scientific disciplines, thrives on diversity of thought. Liskov's unique perspectives and insights have dramatically improved programming languages, making them more accessible and reliable for future generations of programmers.

Throughout her career, Barbara Liskov has received numerous accolades and honors. Beyond the Turing Award, she has been elected to the National Academy of Engineering and the American Academy of Arts and Sciences. These honors reflect not just her technical prowess but her role as a transformative figure in computer science.

Moreover, her approach to problem-solving and innovation has always been deeply pragmatic. By focusing on creating real-world solutions and practical applications for her theoretical insights, Liskov bridged the gap between academia and industry. This pragmatic approach not only earned her widespread respect but also ensured that her work had far-reaching implications beyond the confines of research laboratories.

Today, Barbara Liskov continues to inspire new generations of computer scientists. Her contributions serve as a reminder that the evolution of programming languages is not just a technical challenge but a creative endeavor that requires imaginative thinking and a willingness to question existing norms. Her work continues to influence educational curricula, ensuring that young computer scientists are versed in the principles of robust and reliable software design.

In a world increasingly driven by software, the importance of Liskov's contributions cannot be overemphasized. Her pioneering research in programming languages laid a foundation that modern software engineering builds upon every day. By emphasizing clarity, reliability, and efficiency in code, she has enabled the creation of complex systems that power everything from everyday applications to critical infrastructure.

The story of Barbara Liskov is as much about the evolution of programming languages as it is about the evolution of a discipline that benefits from diverse voices and perspectives. Her legacy is enduring, not just in the code that runs our devices but in the inspiration she provides to those daring to imagine a more inclusive and innovative future in technology.

Thus, Liskov's career is a beacon for aspiring computer scientists, especially women. Her journey encourages them to delve into research and innovation, to break through barriers, and to contribute to fields traditionally dominated by men. As we look to the future, it's evident that Liskov's foundations in programming languages will continue to be a vital part of the technological landscape, inspiring advancements for years to come.

Radia Perlman: The Mother of the Internet

When we trace the intricate web of the modern Internet, few names stand out as vibrantly or as critically as Radia Perlman's. She is often hailed as "The Mother of the Internet," a title that conveys her colossal contribution to the network technologies that underpin our digital lives. Her invention of the Spanning Tree Protocol (STP) in the 1980s became a cornerstone of network design, allowing for the growth and scalability of Ethernet networks.

Born in 1951, Radia grew up in a time when the notion of a networked world was more science fiction than reality. But she was captivated by the early computers she encountered. In high school, frequenting the Computer Club, she experienced firsthand the frustrating limitations of the technology of the time. She attended MIT, majoring in mathematics and later focusing on computer science. Here she not only honed her technical skills but also developed the resilience necessary to thrive in a male-dominated field.

Radia's professional journey led her to Digital Equipment Corporation (DEC), where her work on network protocols would redefine the way we think about data flow and connectivity. While the technical specifications of her work are intricate, the impact is simply massive. STP eliminated data loops in network systems, a problem that could cause entire networks to crash. Imagine the digital chaos without Perlman's solution: We take for granted flawless data delivery, thanks to her ingenuity.

Her career, however, was not without its challenges. The tech industry in the late 20th century was a gauntlet of gender biases and systemic obstacles. Radia faced these adversities not just with resolve, but also with innovation. She remained undeterred by skepticism and questions about her intellectual capacities, instead letting her groundbreaking achievements speak volumes.

Success did not make her rest on her laurels. Perlman's thirst for knowledge and passion for improvement saw her contribute to other essential protocols and technologies as well. She participated in the development of IS-IS and TRILL, both of which have become integral to modern network architectures. Her work essentially laid down the pathways and firelines through which our complex digital habitats are constructed today.

One of Perlman's most inspiring qualities is her unyielding belief in simplicity and elegance in design. She once said, "The purpose of art is expression; the purpose of engineering is invention." This statement encapsulates her philosophy that engineering solutions should be straightforward, usable, and impactful. Despite achieving mastery over highly complex systems, Radia always emphasized the importance of making technology accessible.

Her written contributions, particularly "Interconnections: Bridges, Routers, Switches, and Internetworking Protocols," have become seminal texts for anyone delving into the world of networking. The book is renowned for breaking down convoluted concepts into digestible, understandable ideas. This only bolsters her legacy, making her not just a pioneer but also an educator and mentor to countless aspiring
engineers.

Furthermore, Radia's work extends beyond just protocol development. She has mentored many young engineers and advocated for inclusivity in tech. Her influence is evident in the numerous awards and recognitions bestowed upon her, including her induction into the National Inventors Hall of Fame and the Internet Hall of Fame. Each accolade is a testament to both her prodigious talent and unflagging dedication.

It's easy to overlook the human side behind these towering achievements. Radia is also an accomplished pianist and juggler, embodying a multidimensional persona that defies the stereotypical image of a tech geek. Her diverse interests not only exemplify her versatility but also highlight an essential lesson: great minds find balance in variety.

Finally, one can't discuss Radia Perlman without touching on her role as a mother—a role she navigated alongside her professional duties with extraordinary grace. Balancing parenthood with a demanding career in tech exemplifies her incredible ability to manage multiple high-stakes responsibilities. Her story offers inspiration to women everywhere, demonstrating that it's possible to sculpt a thriving career without sacrificing other vital facets of life.

Radia's journey serves as a beacon for all aspiring engineers navigating the daunting landscape of technology. Her persistence, passion, and brilliance carve a path forward, highlighting that the next generation of tech pioneers can dare to dream big. She demonstrates that with resilience, ingenuity, and a dedication to one's craft, it's possible to leave an indelible mark on the world.

As the digital landscape continues to evolve and expand, Radia Perlman's contributions will remain cornerstones of how we communicate, share, and connect. Future generations of tech enthusiasts, feminists, and engineers will look back on her work, drawing inspiration to push boundaries, challenge norms, and innovate boldly. Her

legacy proves that the seemingly impossible can be achieved and transformed into the indispensable.

CHAPTER 6:
TECH ENTREPRENEURS

In the realm of tech entrepreneurship, vision and resilience intersect to shape transformative journeys. Trailblazers such as Susan Kare and Meg Whitman turned innovative ideas into industry benchmarks, displaying an unyielding commitment to revolutionizing technology. Kare's groundbreaking work in designing the iconic graphical interface for Apple transformed the way we interact with computers, making technology accessible and engaging for millions. Meanwhile, Whitman's unparalleled leadership at eBay and later at HP showcases her strategic acumen and ability to steer colossal enterprises through periods of significant growth and innovation. Their stories imbue an inspiring sense of possibility, illustrating how uncharted paths can lead to monumental successes, especially for women who dare to dream and persist in an industry often marred by gender disparity.

Susan Kare: Designing Icons for Apple

In 1982, a young artist named Susan Kare was introduced to an entirely new world. At the time, Apple was striving to make computing accessible and intuitive, a vision that depended upon the creation of a user-friendly graphical interface. Little did anyone know, Susan Kare would be instrumental in shaping this vision through her innovative icon designs.

At Apple, Kare's mission was clear but daunting: to create icons that would translate complex computer commands into intuitive, visual cues. Her art background played an essential role in this task. She wasn't just designing for functionality; she was imbuing these icons with personality and simplicity. Kare's work at Apple challenged the traditional boundaries of what art could be, transforming it into a tool for user experience.

Kare's design philosophy was both groundbreaking and deeply empathetic. Her goal was to make computers less intimidating for the average person. When she created the smiling "Happy Mac" icon, which greeted users upon starting their Macintosh computers, she was doing more than just drawing a face; she was creating a friendly experience that humanized technology.

One of her most iconic creations, the "command" key symbol, demonstrates her innovative thinking. Apple needed a symbol for a key that would perform multiple functions, and Kare drew inspiration from a Swedish campground sign representing a place of interest. This blend of cultural references and practical functionality is a hallmark of Kare's design genius.

In addition to their practical utility, Kare's icons were remarkable for their almost instinctive familiarity. The trash can for "delete," the diskette for "save," and the paintbrush for "draw" are all examples of how she used easy-to-understand imagery to make the digital world accessible. These icons are still in use today, a testament to their enduring relevance.

Her methods were as innovative as her designs. Kare manually created her icons on graph paper before transferring them to the computer. This painstaking process required an eye for detail and a vision for how these designs would look on tiny, low-resolution screens. The fact that her creations were effective on such a limited canvas speaks to her exceptional skill and creativity.

Susan Kare didn't consider herself a "techie," but her contributions to Apple's Macintosh were revolutionary. By making computers user-friendly and visually appealing, she played a crucial role in democratizing technology. Her work made it possible for everyday people to interact with complex machines naturally and intuitively, setting the stage for the personal computing revolution.

Her influence extended beyond the Macintosh. Microsoft's Windows operating system, for example, employed some of Kare's icon designs, demonstrating her broader impact on personal computing. Her work transcended brand loyalty and industry rivalries; it was about improving how humans interacted with machines, no matter the platform.

Moreover, Kare's design approach was fundamentally user-centered, a concept that was relatively new at the time. She focused on understanding users' needs and crafting visual solutions to address them. This focus on empathy and practicality is a guiding principle in today's user-experience design field, illustrating her lasting contribution to the industry.

Understanding Susan Kare's contribution to technology involves looking beyond the icons themselves to see the broader narrative. She represents a powerful intersection of art and technology, showcasing how creative talents can solve technical challenges. Her story offers an inspiring example for aspiring female engineers and tech enthusiasts, reminding them that diverse skills and perspectives can lead to groundbreaking innovations.

Despite her profound impact, Kare remained remarkably humble about her achievements. She often credited her colleagues and the collaborative environment at Apple for her success. This humility, combined with her trailblazing work, makes her an exemplary figure in the tech industry.

For feminists, Kare's story has particular resonance. Women were underrepresented in the tech field during her time at Apple—not unlike today. Yet, she carved out her space and significantly influenced the company's direction, paving the way for future generations of women in technology.

Inspiring figures like Susan Kare show that there is no single path to success in tech. Her background in fine arts might have seemed unconventional for a tech role, but it was precisely this unique perspective that made her work so exceptional. This reinforces the idea that diverse experiences and skills can lead to extraordinary achievements in any field.

Susan Kare is a testament to the power of creativity and empathy in solving complex problems. Her work has not only left an indelible mark on technology but has also shown that great design is about more than aesthetics; it's about making the world a better place through thoughtful and user-centric solutions.

Meg Whitman: From eBay to HP

Meg Whitman's journey from eBay to HP is a story of transformative leadership and undeniable grit. For aspiring female engineers and tech enthusiasts alike, her career serves as a compelling example of what happens when ambition meets opportunity and a relentless drive for excellence.

Born Margaret Cushing Whitman, Meg started her professional journey away from tech. With an impressive academic background, boasting degrees from Princeton University and Harvard Business School, she initially entered the world of consumer goods, working at Procter & Gamble and later at Disney, Hasbro, and Stride Rite. Little did she know that these varied experiences were preparing her for a monumental shift in her career.

In 1998, Meg Whitman's career took a pivotal turn when she joined eBay as CEO. At that time, the online auction platform was a fledgling startup with just 30 employees. Understanding both the power and the peril of the internet, Whitman was tasked with transforming eBay into a reliable marketplace. She did this with remarkable acumen, focusing on community and trust-building.

"I wanted to work on something that would change people's lives," Whitman has often said. At eBay, that ethos became palpable in every strategic decision she made. Under her leadership, eBay grew from earning roughly $4 million in revenue to $8 billion. With her emphasis on robust user experiences and streamlined processes, Whitman transformed eBay from a quirky auction site into a global e-commerce titan.

But her achievements at eBay were only the beginning. In 2011, Whitman assumed the role of CEO at HP, a storied but struggling tech giant with a history that dated back to a Palo Alto garage. HP was in turmoil; its business model was fractured, its workforce demoralized, and its relevance questioned in a rapidly evolving tech landscape. Many doubted her ability to turn things around.

Whitman tackled HP's challenges head-on. She initiated a five-year turnaround plan, focusing on innovation, restructuring, and separating the company's many divisions to better focus on core strengths. The results weren't immediate. Yet, with a steadfast approach to execution, she managed to split HP into Hewlett Packard Enterprise (HPE) and HP Inc. This move allowed each division to focus on their specific markets—servers/cloud solutions and personal systems/printing, respectively.

Her leadership at HP showcased her ability to make tough decisions. In an industry often dominated by men, Whitman's decisions weren't just about steering a corporate behemoth; they were about redefining what strong, decisive leadership looked like. It was a leadership style grounded in transparency, communication, and a scientific approach to problem-solving. Her decisions were data-driven but also infused with her unique human touch—qualities often attributed to her success at eBay.

Whitman didn't just stop at financial restructuring; she made it a point to foster a more inclusive and diversified workforce. Understanding that technological innovation thrives in diverse environments, she prioritized hiring women and minorities, enriching HP's work culture and broadening its innovative potential.

Beyond her role in corporate boardrooms, Whitman also has a remarkable political career. She ran for the governor of California in 2010, securing the Republican nomination. Although she did not win, her gubernatorial campaign raised her profile and demonstrated her willingness to step out of her comfort zone to effect change.

Her transition from eBay to HP exemplifies a dynamic interplay between consistency and adaptability. At eBay, she laid the groundwork for a company's meteoric rise by focusing on community and scalable technology. At HP, she set the stage for rejuvenation through resource realignment, all while managing to keep stakeholders on board through transparent, effective communication.

Interestingly, Whitman's career offers multiple lessons that apply beyond corporate settings. For feminists and aspiring female tech entrepreneurs, her rise through predominantly male-dominated industries serves as proof that leadership requires neither the loudest voice nor the most forceful demeanor. Instead, it embraces qualities such as empathy, persistence, and a willingness to listen and learn.

Meg Whitman's legacy isn't merely about balance sheets and stock prices. It stretches far into the realm of social change, diversity advocacy, and the reshaping of corporate landscapes to be more inclusive and forward-thinking. Her professional journey from eBay to HP is not just a narrative of career progression but a lesson in transformative leadership fueled by vision, empathy, and relentless dedication.

Ultimately, Whitman exemplifies a blend of traditional business acumen with innovative thinking, qualities that have propelled her into the annals of inspirational tech leadership. Her journey is far from over, and with each role, she continues to inspire the next generation of tech entrepreneurs to reach beyond conventional wisdom and embrace the extraordinary possibilities that lie ahead.

CHAPTER 7:
CYBERSECURITY CHAMPIONS

In the realm of cybersecurity, where the stakes are perpetually high, two trailblazers stand out for their groundbreaking contributions: Joan Clarke and Margaret Hamilton. Joan Clarke, whose codebreaking prowess at Bletchley Park during World War II, played an instrumental role in decrypting enemy communications, thereby altering the course of history. Her story is a testament to the power of intellect and resilience in a field dominated by secrecy and urgency. Similarly, Margaret Hamilton's work on the Apollo software not only screamed innovation but also etched her name in the annals of technology, as her meticulous coding ensured the safety and success of moon missions. These women's achievements underline the critical importance of cybersecurity expertise and the exceptional impact that determined individuals can have on global events and technological advances.

Joan Clarke: Codebreaking at Bletchley Park

Amidst the rolling hills of Buckinghamshire in England, during the throes of World War II, a young woman walked into one of the most secretive and consequential workplaces in the world—Bletchley Park. Joan Clarke, a brilliant mathematician, was about to embark on a path that would not only challenge her intellect but also defy societal norms. Her contributions to breaking the Enigma code would play a pivotal role in the Allied victory and earn her a place among the most revered figures in cybersecurity history.

Born in London in 1917, Clarke's early academic achievements foreshadowed the extraordinary impact she would later have. She attended Newnham College, Cambridge, here she received top honors in mathematics, despite the institutional limitations placed on women that barred her from officially receiving a degree. Those accolades, however, were enough to catch the attention of Gordon Welchman, a key figure in British cryptographic efforts at the time. Clarke was soon recruited to join a select group of codebreakers at Bletchley Park, a decision that would pivot the war in favor of the Allies.

Clarke's role at Bletchley Park was nothing short of transformative. She joined Hut 8, a section led by the renowned Alan Turing, and quickly demonstrated her mathematical prowess. Initially tasked with more straightforward clerical work, she soon earned her stripes working directly on the Naval Enigma—the complex German cipher that had stymied even the best cryptographers. Turing, recognizing her genius, made her one of the few women employed as a full-fledged cryptanalyst. With this opportunity, Clarke not only broke codes but also broke through gender barriers that would pave the way for future generations of women in technology.

The work at Bletchley Park was grueling, often requiring long hours in cold, dimly lit rooms, where the faint hum of Enigma machines provided the soundtrack to lives lived in secrecy. Clarke, however, thrived under these conditions. Her ability to grasp intricate mathematical problems, combined with an uncanny knack for lateral thinking, made her an invaluable asset. While the specifics of her contributions remain cloaked in secrecy even today, it is widely acknowledged that she played a key role in deciphering messages that saved countless lives and shortened the war by years.

In an era where women were largely relegated to supportive roles, Joan Clarke emerged as a leader and pioneer. Her collaboration with Turing extended beyond professional realms; the two shared a close bond, one that saw them briefly engaged to be married. While their romantic relationship was ultimately short-lived, their professional synergy yielded groundbreaking results. Clarke's systematic approach complemented Turing's innovative algorithms, creating a formidable duo whose legacy would resonate far beyond the war.

Clarke's work was largely conducted in anonymity—an unfortunate but not uncommon reality for many women in tech at the time. Nonetheless, her name today commands respect and admiration. Her story captivates not just because of her intellectual achievements, but also because of her quiet defiance against the gendered roles imposed by society. Clarke never sought fame; she sought results, and in doing so, became an unwilling yet iconic figure in the annals of cybersecurity.

Her post-war years were spent continuing her work in cryptography for the Government Communications Headquarters (GCHQ). Her contributions during this period remain classified but are believed to have significantly advanced the field. Despite the lack of public recognition during her lifetime, Clarke received several accolades posthumously, underscoring the magnitude of her contributions to both the war effort and the development of modern cryptographic methods.

Joan Clarke's life is a testament to the power of intellectual curiosity, resilience, and quiet determination. Her achievements at Bletchley Park serve as a poignant reminder that brilliance knows no gender. For aspiring female engineers and tech enthusiasts, Clarke's journey offers an inspiring narrative of overcoming obstacles and redefining what is possible. Her legacy calls upon each of us to question the limitations set before us and to realize that the potential for greatness resides within all, regardless of societal constraints.

Today, as we confront new and sophisticated challenges in the realm of cybersecurity, Joan Clarke's contributions serve as a bedrock upon which modern efforts are built. She stood shoulder to shoulder with some of the greatest minds of her time and made indelible marks on the very fabric of modern cryptography. Her story isn't just one of breaking codes; it's a story of breaking through—through the fog of war, through the barriers of gender, and through the constraints of recognition.

In reflecting on Clarke's legacy, it becomes evident that her impact was not confined to a single era or task. She exemplified the kind of perseverance and ingenuity that continue to inspire today's tech innovators. For those women who aspire to leave their mark in tech, Joan Clarke stands as a beacon of what can be achieved through dedication, skill, and unyielding commitment. As we honor her contributions, we are reminded that the fight for recognition and equality in tech is ongoing, and that true cybersecurity champions, like Clarke, continue to inspire and lead the way.

Margaret Hamilton: Apollo's Software Screamer

The name Margaret Hamilton resonates powerfully among those familiar with the Apollo space missions. As the lead software engineer for NASA's Apollo program, she was at the helm of many of the critical operations that brought humankind to the moon. Yet, her contributions go far beyond her technical prowess; they weave into the broader tapestry of what's possible when one combines genius with resilience. Her work stands as a testament to the logical yet innovative pathways minds can traverse, even when faced with the most daunting technological challenges.

Born in 1936, Hamilton's journey into the world of software engineering was as unconventional as it was inspiring. She initially pursued a degree in mathematics, a field that was just beginning to crack open windows into the limitless possibilities of computing. Hamilton's intelligence was evident, but her career took an unexpected turn when she found a position working on software reliability for the SAGE project. This early experience laid the groundwork for her future accomplishments at NASA.

In the early 1960s, the landscape of computing was quite different from what it is today. Computers were room-sized behemoths that required intricate knowledge to operate. Software engineering, as a discipline, didn't even exist. Margaret Hamilton didn't just work within these limitations; she helped define the field itself. She coined the term "software engineering" at a time when her contributions were critically shaping its parameters.

Hamilton joined MIT's Charles Stark Draper Laboratory, where she was tasked with developing the onboard software for the Apollo missions. It wasn't a title earned easily, nor without its struggles. The stakes were high; the software had to be flawless. There could be no room for error. Imagine the weight of responsibility, knowing that any glitch or misstep could result in catastrophe. But Hamilton was undeterred. She gathered a team and established rigorous protocols, spearheading a movement toward reliable software engineering principles.

In the midst of all the technological hurdles, it was Hamilton's human touch that often stood out. She approached her team not just as programmers but as thinkers, strategists, and problem-solvers. She understood that good software wasn't just about code; it was about creating systems that could anticipate and mitigate human error. This philosophy reached its zenith during the Apollo 11 mission when an unexpected error 1202 alarm threatened the entire lunar landing.

As Neil Armstrong and Buzz Aldrin prepared for their descent, the Apollo Guidance Computer began to overload with data. Anxious moments passed as the astronauts awaited instructions from Earth. Hamilton's foresight had included safeguards for such a scenario. The system was designed to prioritize crucial tasks, allowing the mission to proceed without jeopardy. This error management became a pivotal moment in space history, demonstrating the critical importance of fail-safe software design.

But why were these alarms going off? To the untrained eye, it might have seemed like an oversight. Hamilton knew better. The computer, a marvel of its time, had limited processing power and storage. Nevertheless, it was robust enough to manage the complexities of the mission thanks to Hamilton's meticulous planning. Each line of code was scrutinized, each algorithm subjected to rigorous testing. The Apollo 11 moon landing would forever be a landmark achievement, underscored by the invisible yet indispensable contributions of Hamilton and her team.

In recognizing her influence, it's essential to consider the environment in which Hamilton thrived. The 1960s and 1970s weren't particularly hospitable to women in technology. Hamilton faced skepticism and was often the only woman in the room. Yet, she holds a mirror to every aspiring female engineer, reflecting that one's gender does not determine one's potential. Her career reminds us that brilliance acknowledges no boundaries.

Hamilton's contributions continued to extend beyond NASA. After her stint with the space program, she founded Hamilton Technologies, Inc., where she developed Universal Systems Language (USL). This language was designed to elevate the reliability of complex software systems, further embedding her legacy in the realm of safe and reliable software engineering. It's not merely a footnote in her career but an expanding legacy that continues to impact various fields, from aviation to healthcare.

Her accolades are fittingly numerous. In 2003, Hamilton received NASA's Exceptional Space Act Award, and in 2016, she was awarded the Presidential Medal of Freedom. Each award serves as an acknowledgment of the broader implications of her work. Her story isn't just about landing on the moon; it's about elevating the boundaries of what software engineering could achieve. It's about steering a field from its infancy into a critical domain of modern technology.

Margaret Hamilton's life is a vivid blend of intellect, courage, and foresight. Her role in the Apollo missions isn't just an episode of historical significance; it's a continuing saga that touches upon how we perceive and handle technology today. She has set a cornerstone for future generations of engineers, inventors, and dreamers. Her story inspires us not just to reach for the stars but to consider carefully the paths and safeguards we create along the way.

In examining the broader canvas, her achievements emphasize something fundamental: Technology is not merely about advancement but about human ingenuity and empathy. Her meticulousness and concern for the safety of the astronauts reflect a deep-seated understanding that behind every machine, every line of code, is a human life that depends on it.

Have we come far from those room-sized computers? Yes. But the spirit of innovation, the quest for reliability, and the courage to venture into the unknown remain constants in the story of technology. And in that narrative, Margaret Hamilton's voice is not just a chapter but a defining tone, urging us to dream ambitiously and design diligently.

As we advance, developing artificial intelligence and exploring Mars, Hamilton's principles will guide us. Designing for reliability, anticipating error, promoting inclusivity in tech—these are not just best practices. They are imperatives grounded in her legacy. Margaret Hamilton has shown us that to be a true champion in cybersecurity and software engineering, one must marry skill with foresight, and innovation with responsibility.

CHAPTER 8:
PUSHING THE LIMITS OF AI

Artificial Intelligence isn't just a technological marvel; it's a frontier that's constantly being redefined by visionaries like Fei-Fei Li and Cynthia Breazeal. These pioneering women challenge the boundaries of what's possible, helping machines see with human-like vision and interact socially with empathy and intelligence. Their work not only advances AI but also reshapes our understanding of it, making it an integral part of our lives. They're testing the limits, smashing stereotypes, and inspiring the next generation of female engineers to think beyond what's already known. In everything from medical diagnostics to robotic companions, their contributions illuminate a path where imagination and innovation meet, proving that the future of AI isn't just about algorithms and data—it's about human potential realized through relentless curiosity and dedication.

Fei-Fei Li: Bringing Vision to Machines

Fei-Fei Li isn't just a name in the field of artificial intelligence; she's a revolver of a paradigm. As an AI pioneer, Fei-Fei's work can be credited for transforming the landscape of machine learning and computer vision. Her enthusiasm and dedication have contributed to the development of technologies that can see and understand the world as humans do. For tech enthusiasts and aspiring engineers, Fei-Fei's story is a beacon of what passion and perseverance can achieve.

Born in Beijing and moved to the United States at the age of sixteen, Fei-Fei showcased an insatiable curiosity and keen intellect from an early age. Straddling two cultures, she combined the rigorous discipline of her Chinese upbringing with the innovative spirit of the American educational system. This blend of influences would later infuse her work with a rare depth and global perspective. However, it was not an easy journey. Armed with unwavering support from her parents, she battled through the language barrier and societal challenges without losing focus on her dream.

One can't discuss Fei-Fei Li without mentioning ImageNet, the revolutionary project that she spearheaded. In 2007, Fei-Fei and her team began compiling the ImageNet database, a mammoth collection of over 14 million annotated images across more than 20,000 categories. The goal was ambitious: to improve image recognition software so drastically that machines would be able to see and comprehend the world. This enormous undertaking required not just technical acumen, but also remarkable leadership and project management skills.

Why was ImageNet groundbreaking? Before its inception, computer vision was limited by the inadequacy of training data. For machines to understand visuals, they needed comprehensive and well-annotated data to learn from. ImageNet provided just that—a treasure trove of data that allowed researchers worldwide to train and refine image recognition algorithms, leading to significant advancements in AI. In the years following its release, ImageNet played a crucial role in the development of deep learning algorithms, pushing the boundaries of what's possible.

Fei-Fei's contribution goes beyond technology; it marks a change in how we perceive the relationship between machines and the world. She brought an empathetic touch to this otherwise cold, clinical field. Through her work, she emphasized that artificial intelligence is not about creating superhumans, but about augmenting human capabilities and making our lives better. In many of her talks, she passionately discusses how AI can solve societal challenges, from healthcare improvements to environmental sustainability.

Working tirelessly as a professor at Stanford University, Fei-Fei has also shown deep commitment to fostering the next generation of engineers and innovators. She co-founded the Stanford Human-Centered AI Institute, advocating for a holistic approach to AI that integrates technical advancements with social impact. For Fei-Fei, it's not just about machines; it's about people and how machines can serve humanity in meaningful ways.

Speaking of inspiration, Fei-Fei's journey holds a mirror to aspiring female engineers and feminists alike. In an industry plagued by gender disparity, she stands tall as a figure of representation, proving that women can lead groundbreaking projects and make substantial contributions to technology. She has often been vocal about the necessity of diversity in AI, stressing that a broad range of perspectives leads to more ethical and balanced technological advancements.

But Fei-Fei's story isn't just about overcoming professional challenges; it's also a testimony to personal perseverance. Her path was strewn with obstacles common to female scientists. She faced skepticism and bias but refused to be daunted. Instead of seeing these barriers as roadblocks, she viewed them as hurdles to be surmounted, using each challenge as an opportunity to grow and learn.

Fei-Fei's narrative is one that involves endless hours of work balanced with personal commitments. Her life is a study in time management and dedication, a reminder that excellence often requires sacrifices and relentless effort. Yet, despite the intense demands of her career, Fei-Fei has always prioritized mentoring and inspiring others, particularly young women and minorities in tech.

Her leadership style is another facet worth examining. Fei-Fei believes in servant leadership, making space for her team's voices to be heard and fostering an environment where creativity and innovation can thrive. She integrates empathy and assertiveness in her leadership style, ensuring her team feels valued and motivated. This approach has not only driven the success of her projects but has also cultivated a culture of respect and collaboration often missing in tech environments.

Fei-Fei Li's influence extends into policy and ethics as well. Recognizing the profound societal implications of AI, she frequently engages in dialogues about the ethical applications of AI technologies. Her work underscores the importance of aligning AI advancements with human values and ethics. She has spoken extensively on the need for policies that ensure AI benefits society at large and does not exacerbate existing inequalities.

Though Fei-Fei is celebrated for her technical contributions, it's her humanistic approach that sets her apart. She's a strong advocate for the ethical development of AI, emphasizing that technology should work for social good. This perspective has invited collaborations with interdisciplinary teams, including psychologists, sociologists, and medical professionals, highlighting her belief in the interconnectedness of technology and society.

Looking forward, Fei-Fei remains an indefatigable force in AI research and advocacy. Her vision for the future extends beyond the laboratory to classrooms, boardrooms, and policy forums. She envisions a world where AI not only advances technology but also enhances human life, promoting health, education, and well-being. As AI continues to evolve, Fei-Fei's emphasis on a human-centered approach will remain a guiding principle, steering the conversation towards more inclusive and ethical technological advancements.

Fei-Fei Li's legacy is multifaceted—she's a scientist, an advocate, a leader, and a mentor. Her story affirms that vision and persistence can indeed push the boundaries of what's possible. She reminds us that while technology holds incredible potential, it's the human element—

compassion, ethics, and empathy—that gives it true meaning and direction. For anyone seeking inspiration in the realm of technology or the broader spectrum of life, Fei-Fei Li's journey is a testament to what's achievable when vision meets action.

Cynthia Breazeal: Pioneer of Social Robots

Cynthia Breazeal is not just a scientist; she is a visionary who dared to redefine the relationship between humans and machines. As one of the most influential figures in the world of robotics and artificial intelligence, Breazeal's work has pushed the boundaries of what robots can do and, more importantly, how they can interact with us. Her groundbreaking work in the field of social robotics has paved the way for a new era where robots are not just tools or automated systems but companions and assistants.

From a young age, Breazeal showed an insatiable curiosity about the world around her. This inquisitiveness drove her to pursue a career in electrical engineering and computer science, fields she saw as key to unlocking the future. Her academic journey took her to the Massachusetts Institute of Technology (MIT), where she earned a bachelor's degree in electrical and computer engineering, followed by a PhD in the same field. It was here, at MIT, that Breazeal's fascination with robotics truly took flight.

Breazeal's doctoral thesis became the foundation for her lifelong work in social robotics. She introduced Kismet, a robot designed to interact and communicate with humans through expressive facial features and emotional responses. Kismet wasn't just a technological marvel; it was a groundbreaking piece of engineering that challenged the conventional wisdom about human-robot interaction. For the first time, a robot could engage people in a way that felt natural, warm, and humane.

"We like the idea of a robot being more than just a machine," Breazeal has often said. "Robots should be able to connect with us on an emotional level, making our interactions with them more meaningful and effective." Kismet was a living testament to this philosophy, showcasing how emotional intelligence could be integrated into robotic systems. The research and development that went into Kismet laid the groundwork for future advancements in the field of social robotics.

Following the success of Kismet, Breazeal founded the Personal Robots Group at the MIT Media Lab. Her team focused on developing robots that could serve as interactive characters and assistive devices. This marked a significant shift from the traditional view in robotics, where the primary aim was to enhance efficiency and productivity. Instead, Breazeal's work emphasized the robot's ability to understand, interpret, and respond to human emotions and social cues. By doing so, she opened up new possibilities for robots to assist in education, healthcare, and even companionship.

One of Breazeal's notable contributions is the creation of Jibo, a social robot designed for home use. Marketed as "the first social robot for the home," Jibo was capable of doing more than just responding to commands. It could recognize the faces and voices of different household members, engage in playful banter, and even participate in family activities. Jibo represented a new class of consumer robots, embodying Breazeal's vision of machines that are integrated seamlessly into our daily lives, improving our quality of life through emotional and social intelligence.

Breazeal's work extends beyond academic settings and commercial products. She has also been a strong advocate for ethical AI and responsible innovation. Conscious of the potential ethical dilemmas posed by advanced robotics and AI systems, she has emphasized the importance of designing technologies that are not just intelligent but also ethical and beneficial for society. She has participated in numerous panels, conferences, and advisory boards to discuss and promote responsible AI practices, ensuring that the development of these technologies remains aligned with human values.

What sets Breazeal apart is her unwavering commitment to bridging the gap between machines and humans. Her pioneering efforts in social robotics have underscored the importance of empathy, emotional intelligence, and ethical considerations in the development of AI technologies. Unlike many of her contemporaries who focus on technical prowess alone, Breazeal envisions a future where robots are an integral part of the human social fabric — not just efficient assistants but compassionate companions who understand and respond to our emotional needs.

Moreover, Breazeal's influence extends to future generations of engineers and technologists. Through her role as an educator, she has inspired countless students to explore the fields of AI and robotics, encouraging them to think creatively about the societal impacts of their work. Her courses at MIT are known for their interdisciplinary approach, combining elements of engineering, psychology, and social sciences to offer a holistic view of robotics.

Breazeal's ability to fuse technical innovation with a deep understanding of human psychology has made her a role model not just for aspiring engineers but also for those who advocate for more inclusive and empathetic technology. She has been a vocal supporter of increasing diversity in tech spaces, particularly encouraging women to pursue careers in STEM fields. Her success and leadership serve as a powerful testament to what can be achieved when creativity, empathy, and technical expertise come together.

Cynthia Breazeal's work is a testament to the transformative power of interdisciplinary thinking. By combining engineering with psychology, social sciences, and ethics, she has created a unique and impactful body of work that continues to influence how we think about and interact with robots. Her social robots are more than mere mechanical marvels; they are harbingers of a future where machines are integrated into our social ecosystems, helping us to live richer, more connected lives.

As we look to the future, the questions Breazeal has raised about the ethical use of AI and the role of robots in society become even more pertinent. How can we ensure that robots serve to enhance human well-being rather than detract from it? What kind of regulations and guidelines should be in place to govern the use of social robots? These are the challenging yet essential questions that Breazeal's work encourages us to ponder.

In many ways, Cynthia Breazeal's journey has just begun. She continues to push the limits of what is possible in the realm of social robotics, challenging both technological and societal norms. Her work reminds us that the true potential of AI lies not just in its ability to perform tasks but in its capacity to connect with us on a deeply human level.

Breazeal's story is one of relentless curiosity, meaningful innovation, and an unwavering commitment to bettering the human experience. She stands as a beacon for anyone who believes in the power of technology to change the world — not just by making our lives easier but by making them richer and more fulfilling.

Through her pioneering work, Breazeal has shown us that the future of AI isn't just about smarter machines; it's about creating technology that understands, respects, and enhances our humanity. In this ever-evolving landscape, Cynthia Breazeal remains a guiding light, leading us toward a more interconnected and empathetic future.

CHAPTER 9:
INNOVATORS IN GAMING

The gaming industry, often perceived as a dominion of male ingenuity, has been irrevocably transformed by pioneering women who dared to envision beyond the status quo. Carol Shaw, one of the first female video game designers, shattered stereotypes with her groundbreaking work like the iconic "River Raid". Meanwhile, Roberta Williams fundamentally reshaped storytelling in gaming with her seminal contributions, including the famed "King's Quest" series. These trailblazers not only designed games but created immersive worlds that captivated millions, proving that innovation transcends gender. Their achievements serve as powerful beacons, guiding future generations of women toward boundless possibilities in the gaming universe. By challenging norms and infusing imagination with technical prowess, they've not only carved out their own legacies but have also paved the way for many to follow.

Carol Shaw: The Original Game Designer

When discussing trailblazing figures in the gaming industry, one can't overlook Carol Shaw. Often heralded as the first female video game designer, Shaw's journey is nothing short of inspiring. Born in 1955 in Palo Alto, California, she grew up in the heart of what would later become Silicon Valley. Surrounded by technology from a young age, Shaw demonstrated an early aptitude for math and science, a talent that later paved the way for her groundbreaking work in gaming.

Carol Shaw's educational background laid the foundation for her illustrious career. She attended the University of California, Berkeley, where she earned her bachelor's degree in electrical engineering and computer science in 1977 and followed it up with a master's degree. This academic achievement was notable during a time when the engineering field was overwhelmingly male-dominated. Her success in these programs proved her remarkable talent and determination to break through gender barriers.

Shaw's entry into the professional world began at Atari, a company synonymous with the early days of gaming. Joining Atari in 1978, she started working as a microprocessor software programmer. It was here that her creative and technical skills found their true calling. Shaw created "3-D Tic-Tac-Toe" for the Atari 2600, one of the first video games designed by a woman. This project demonstrated her ability to blend logic and creativity, setting her apart in the burgeoning video game industry.

One of Shaw's most iconic contributions came in the form of "River Raid," released in 1982 for the Atari 2600. This game not only cemented her legacy but also showcased her exceptional talent in game design and development. River Raid stood out for its innovative gameplay and design, challenging players with its scrolling shooter format and dynamic flight paths. It quickly became a best-seller and is remembered fondly by gamers to this day.

At a time when the gaming industry was in its infancy, Shaw's work was nothing short of revolutionary. She was a pioneer, not only for women in gaming but for the industry as a whole. Her ability to create engaging, challenging, and technically sophisticated games broke new ground and set new standards. Shaw's work empowered future generations of female game designers, proving that talent knows no gender.

Carol Shaw's influence extends beyond her programming successes. Her career path inspires many, demonstrating the importance of persistence and passion. Shaw often talked about her experience as a woman in a male-dominated industry, reflecting on the challenges she faced and how she overcame them. Her story serves as a beacon of hope for those who struggle to find their place in tech-oriented fields.

After her years at Atari, Shaw moved to Activision in 1983, further cementing her status as a key figure in game design. Activision, a company founded by former Atari programmers, offered her an environment where creativity and innovation were encouraged. Here, Shaw's skills continued to flourish, and she developed several games that enjoyed commercial success, further establishing her reputation as a leading developer in the industry.

Throughout her career, Shaw received several accolades recognizing her contributions. In 2017, she was awarded the Industry Icon Award at The Game Awards, a testament to her lifelong contributions to gaming. Receiving such recognition underscored her status as a trailblazer and role model, not just for women in gaming, but for anyone pursuing a career in technology.

Despite retiring in the late 1980s, Shaw's legacy continues to influence the gaming industry. Her innovative designs and the barriers she broke down paved the way for the diverse and inclusive environment the industry strives towards today. She remains an inspirational figure, encouraging a new generation of game designers to push the boundaries of what is possible.

Shaw's journey also highlights the importance of representation in STEM fields. Her career encourages young women to pursue their interests in gaming and technology, showing that it's a field where they can innovate and lead. Shaw often emphasizes that passion and dedication are critical components of success, a message that resonates well beyond the confines of the gaming industry.

Moreover, Carol Shaw's story is a crucial reminder of the potential impact one individual can have on an industry's evolution. From her early days at Atari to her groundbreaking work with Activision, Shaw left an indelible mark on the world of gaming. Her story is one of talent, perseverance, and groundbreaking achievements, providing an inspirational blueprint for aspiring game developers everywhere.

As we look forward to the future of gaming, the influence of pioneers like Carol Shaw cannot be overstated. Her innovative approach and dedication laid crucial groundwork, shaping the gaming world into what it is today. For tech enthusiasts, feminists, aspiring engineers, and anyone interested in inspirational real-life stories, Shaw's career offers a vivid, motivational example of what's possible when passion meets talent. Her impact resonates through time, reminding us of the incredible contributions women make in technology, both then and now.

In closing, Carol Shaw epitomizes the spirit of innovation and the relentless pursuit of excellence. Her career serves as a testament to the power of breaking barriers and pushing beyond the conventional. Shaw's legacy continues to inspire countless individuals, ensuring her story remains a vital part of the history and future of gaming.

Roberta Williams: Foundational Adventure Stories

When we talk about the innovators who fundamentally shaped the gaming industry, Roberta Williams stands out as a monumental figure. Her journey from a curious homemaker to a pioneering game designer redefined interactive storytelling and broadened the horizons of what video games could achieve. Roberta's contributions helped lay the bedrock for story-driven adventure games, a genre that continues to capture the imaginations of millions across the globe.

Roberta's entry into the gaming world was almost serendipitous. In 1979, when video games were mostly simplistic and arcane, her husband, Ken Williams, brought home an early Apple II computer. Roberta, who had not been particularly tech-savvy until then, was captivated by a rudimentary game called "Colossal Cave Adventure." The rich and imaginative narrative of the game resonated with her, sparking a revelation. She saw the potential for storytelling in an interactive medium, a potential that was largely untapped at the time.

Drawing from her experience with classical literature and fairy tales, Roberta began developing her own adventure game concepts. Her first game, "Mystery House," released in 1980, was a watershed moment. It wasn't just any game; it was the first graphical adventure game ever made. "Mystery House" allowed players to visualize the environments described in the text, merging narrative and graphics in a manner that was unprecedented. The game was an instant success, selling over 10,000 copies—a phenomenal achievement for its time.

But Roberta's vision didn't stop there. She co-founded Sierra On-Line with her husband Ken, setting the stage for even more ambitious projects. Sierra On-Line quickly became synonymous with quality and innovation in adventure games. Titles such as "King's Quest" series brought lush worlds, intricate puzzles, and compelling stories to life, making players not just participants, but central characters in the gaming experience. Roberta's creative process and her unwavering commitment to narrative intricacy set the gold standard for game design.

The "King's Quest" series, which began in 1984, emerged as one of the most influential adventure game franchises. The series wasn't merely a collection of games; it was an odyssey that invited players into a realm filled with quests that felt both epic and intimate. Roberta's skillful blending of mythology, folklore, and her original storytelling made "King's Quest" a compelling experience for both young and old gamers alike. Her innovative approach placed players in richly rendered worlds where every decision could change the story's outcome, fostering a sense of agency and immersion that was far ahead of its time.

Moreover, Roberta's design philosophy diverged from the mainstream expectations of video games. While many early games focused primarily on scoring points or defeating opponents, Roberta was dedicated to crafting experiences that emphasized narrative and problem-solving. This was more than just a stylistic choice; it was a deliberate strategy to broaden the gaming audience beyond its predominantly male demographic. Her games were inclusive, intricate, and deeply engaging, attracting a diverse array of players and fostering a love for storytelling in games.

Her influence didn't stop in the 1980s. As technology evolved, so too did Roberta's creative aspirations. She embraced new platforms and graphical capabilities, pushing the envelope with each subsequent release. In 1995, she introduced "Phantasmagoria," a game that ventured into mature and horror territories. The game was marked by its full-motion video scenes and adult themes, pushing the boundaries of what video games could represent. It was both a commercial success and a lightning rod for discussions on content in interactive media.

Roberta Williams' role as a trailblazer cannot be understated. She opened doors for a new breed of game designers who saw the medium as a form of artistic and narrative expression. Her influence can be seen in modern story-rich games, which owe a debt to her pioneering work in blending narrative complexity with interactive elements. Notably, many contemporary designers cite Roberta as a primary inspiration, a testament to her lasting impact on the industry.

Furthermore, Roberta's journey holds particular resonance for women in technology. She broke into a predominantly male industry during a time when female developers were an anomaly. Her success challenged preconceived notions about what women could achieve in the tech world, making her a powerful role model for aspiring female engineers and game designers. She showed that creativity and determination could overcome societal barriers, setting a precedent for future generations.

The legacy of Roberta Williams is not just in the games she created but in the paths she paved. The wider gaming community continues to celebrate her contributions, and rightfully so. Her story is a reminder of what is possible when passion meets perseverance. She taught the world that games could be more than just a pastime; they could tell stories that resonates deeply with players, offering experiences that are as emotionally profound as they are intellectually stimulating.

In conclusion, Roberta Williams' story is one of innovation, resilience, and trailblazing achievements. She dared to dream in pixels and narratives, forever changing the landscape of the gaming industry. Her work continues to inspire, resonating through the digital worlds she helped cultivate and in the hearts of those who still embark on adventures, one quest at a time.

CHAPTER 10:
SHAPING OPEN SOURCE

As we dive into the world of open source, we're introduced to two incredible women who've not only shaped how we build software today but also how we collaborate and innovate together. Mitchell Baker's leadership at Mozilla exemplifies the power of community-driven projects that prioritize openness, transparency, and inclusivity. Her commitment to creating a web accessible to all has left an indelible mark on the way we experience the internet. Then there's Kathy Sierra, whose work has empowered countless developers through her engaging and effective educational content. By focusing on making complex concepts approachable, Sierra has inspired a generation of programmers to excel and create. Together, they illustrate the transformative impact of open source philosophy, demonstrating that technology can be a force for good when driven by a collective spirit. These women not only broke barriers but also opened doors for future innovators to build upon their legacies.

Mitchell Baker: Leading the Mozilla Movement

Mitchell Baker's journey is a testament to the power of visionary leadership in the open-source ecosystem. When Baker co-founded the Mozilla Project, she embarked on an ambitious mission: to ensure that the Internet remained a public resource accessible to all. Her work has left an indelible mark on the tech world, fostering innovation and promoting inclusivity through open-source principles.

Baker didn't just find herself in the tech industry; she carved her own path. Balancing her expertise in law and technology, Baker's entry into the Mozilla Project was nothing short of serendipitous. Her legal background equipped her with the skills to navigate the complex terrain of open-source licensing, a crucial component in the birth and growth of the Mozilla browser.

As the Chief Lizard Wrangler, Mitchell Baker assumed a role that was unconventional, yet perfectly suited to her multifaceted skill set. Her vision extended beyond mere market dominance; she sought to cultivate an ethical tech landscape. Under her stewardship, Mozilla rose not only as a technological innovator but as a staunch advocate for user privacy and open web standards.

Baker's leadership was instrumental in transforming Mozilla from a fledgling project into a pioneering force during the early 2000s. At a time when incumbent tech giants dominated the browser market, Mozilla's Firefox browser, with its emphasis on user control and open-source development, became a beacon of hope for a more open internet. Baker's strategic foresight was critical in navigating competitive pressures and commercial interests while staying true to Mozilla's mission of maintaining user-centric values.

One of Baker's most notable achievements was her adept handling of Mozilla's intricate licensing issues. She championed the Mozilla Public License (MPL), ensuring the project's legal foundation supported a robust, collaborative model. The MPL was more than a mere legal document; it was a manifesto for openness, proclaiming that the code written for Mozilla would always be shared and improved upon by an engaged community. Her legal acumen laid the groundwork for this enduring social contract between Mozilla and its contributors.

Mitchell Baker's emphasis on community was not just lip service. She actively engaged with the global community, fostering a grassroots movement of developers, designers, and advocates who contributed to the project's success. Her inclusive approach included localizing Firefox into multiple languages and making it accessible to users around the world. This community-centric strategy was crucial in gaining widespread adoption and international support.

Remarkably, Baker's influence extended beyond Mozilla. She became a powerful advocate for open-source principles across the tech industry. Her speeches and writings emphasize the importance of transparency, collaboration, and ethical responsibility in technological innovation. She catalyzed conversations about these values at industry conferences and forums, encouraging other tech leaders to adopt similarly sustainable approaches.

Mitchell Baker's leadership style is characterized by a unique blend of empathy and resolve. She understood that building a thriving community required not only visionary goals but also an emotional connection with the people working towards those goals. Baker often highlighted personal stories from developers within the community, putting faces to the contributions that collectively drove Mozilla's success. This empathetic approach cultivated a sense of belonging and purpose among community members, which in turn deepened their commitment to the project.

Baker's resilience was put to the test during Mozilla's turbulent periods. Whether facing financial challenges or grappling with internal dissent, her steadfast commitment to Mozilla's core values never wavered. She found innovative solutions to keep the project afloat, including securing strategic partnerships and diversifying revenue streams without compromising the foundational principles of openness and user sovereignty.

Mitchell Baker's impact also resonates strongly within discussions of gender representation in tech. As one of the few women leading a major tech initiative during her time, she broke stereotypes and provided a powerful example for aspiring female engineers and tech leaders. Her success challenged the gender norms of a male-dominated industry, fostering greater inclusivity not only within Mozilla but also in the broader tech community.

Her legacy can be seen in the enduring relevance of Firefox and the continuous contributions of the Mozilla Foundation. Long after her initial tenure, the organization remains a formidable advocate for an open and inclusive internet. Mozilla's commitment to privacy, security, and user empowerment continues to serve as a model for sustainable and ethical tech development, embodying the pioneering spirit that Baker instilled.

Mitchell Baker's story is more than a recount of professional accomplishments; it is an inspiring narrative of how leadership rooted in ethical principles and community spirit can drive monumental change. For tech enthusiasts, her journey underscores the importance of standing firm on values even when navigating competitive landscapes. For aspiring female engineers and feminists, Baker's career is a beacon of what can be achieved through perseverance and visionary leadership.

In commemorating Mitchell Baker's contributions, we also celebrate the lasting impact of her work on shaping a better internet for future generations. Her leadership not only propelled Mozilla to great heights but also set a precedent for how tech innovations should be approached—always with an unwavering commitment to the greater good.

Kathy Sierra: Empowering Developers

Kathy Sierra's journey into the world of software development started not with programming but with a deep understanding of the human brain. Before she became a household name in the tech world, she was a game developer and later an instructor at Sun Microsystems. What set her apart wasn't just her coding prowess but her unique perspective on how developers learn and retain information. She understood that at the core of every line of code written, a human mind was grappling with new concepts and trying to apply them effectively. Her mission: to make the lives of developers easier, more productive, and genuinely enjoyable.

Sierra's approach to teaching programming was radical for its time. While many focused on the complexity and technical depth of languages, she zoomed out and turned the spotlight on user experience. For her, it wasn't enough that software worked; it had to align with how people actually thought and solved problems. This belief culminated in the co-creation of the "Head First" series of books, a groundbreaking set of guides that made learning fun and intuitive. Their immersive, visually rich format defied conventional educational texts, making subjects like Java, PHP, and Design Patterns accessible and engaging.

One of the core principles Sierra introduced was the importance of emotional engagement in learning. She realized that developers often feel overwhelmed by the sheer volume of information they need to master. By weaving storytelling, humor, and visual aids into their books, she and her co-author Bert Bates created a learning environment that was not only effective but also emotionally satisfying. The success of the "Head First" series underscored a crucial point: when learners are engaged on an emotional level, they grasp concepts more quickly and remember them longer.

Sierra didn't stop there. She took her insights further, delving into the psychology of performance and achieving what she called a "flow state" — those moments when a person is so immersed in their work that time seems to disappear. Her blog, "Creating Passionate Users," became a staple for developers worldwide. Through it, she shared practical tips on how to cultivate this elusive state, making coding not just a job but an exhilarating journey. Her posts, rich with insight and backed by cognitive science, transformed how many approached their daily work.

Equally important was her emphasis on the broader developer ecosystem. Sierra understood early on that the tech community thrives on open collaboration and that the health of this ecosystem depends on the well-being of its contributors. She championed the idea that an empowered developer isn't just technically competent but also emotionally resilient. By advocating for mental health, work-life balance, and community support, she helped shift the industry narrative from one of grind and burnout to one of sustainable passion and joy.

Sierra's influence extends beyond her immediate projects. Her work has empowered many who were traditionally marginalized in the tech industry. She became a vocal advocate for diversity and inclusion, recognizing that varied perspectives drive innovation. By fostering a welcoming environment for women, minorities, and those transitioning from non-technical backgrounds, she helped broaden participation in open source communities. Her message was clear: everyone has something valuable to contribute, and the best software arises from diverse teams.

At conferences and workshops, Sierra's talks frequently left audiences invigorated, her energy and enthusiasm proving infectious. She had a unique ability to demystify complex ideas, distilling them into actionable insights. Her sessions weren't just lectures; they were experiences designed to inspire and engage. By the end, attendees often felt more confident in their abilities and more connected to their peers.

Despite her substantial impact, Sierra faced her own share of challenges. Like many women in tech, she encountered skepticism and pushback. However, she met these obstacles with resilience and grace, using them as fuel for her advocacy. Her transparency about these struggles has made her an even more relatable and inspiring figure. By sharing her journey openly, she has allowed others to see that while the path may be difficult, it is navigable, and success is achievable.

In reflecting upon Kathy Sierra's legacy in shaping open source, it's clear that her contributions go beyond the tangible outputs of books and blog posts. She has fundamentally changed how developers view their work and themselves. Her focus on user-friendly design, emotional engagement, and community well-being has sparked a much-needed evolution in the tech industry. Her voice continues to resonate, encouraging developers to not only aim for technical excellence but also personal fulfillment and inclusive practices.

In aspiring to create passionate users, Sierra has, in many ways, created passionate creators. Her emphasis on the human aspects of software development has paved the way for a more empathetic and inclusive tech culture. As we look to the future of open source, her influence remains a guiding light, reminding us that at the core of every successful project is a community that feels valued, inspired, and excited about what lies ahead.

CHAPTER 11:
CHAMPIONS OF INCLUSION

Amidst the transformational waves in the tech industry, Kimberly Bryant and Reshma Saujani shine as beacons of inclusion, showing that the future of technology must embrace diversity to unlock its full potential. Kimberly's groundbreaking initiative, Black Girls CODE, has not only empowered thousands of young girls of color to envision themselves as tech innovators but has also challenged the industry's homogeneous culture. Her efforts resonate deeply, reminding us that the face of innovation is multifaceted. Parallel to this, Reshma Saujani's passionate crusade through Girls Who Code has tirelessly worked to close the gender gap in technology, equipping girls with the skills and confidence to excel in the tech world. Their stories act as rallying cries, urging the tech community to foster environments where every voice, regardless of race or gender, can contribute and thrive. These champions of inclusion are not just reshaping the landscape of tech; they are crafting a more inclusive future, driven by a belief that diversity is the cornerstone of true innovation.

Kimberly Bryant: Changing the Face of Tech with Black Girls CODE

Among the many remarkable individuals who have championed diversity in the tech industry, Kimberly Bryant stands out as a transformative figure. Her journey, marked by perseverance and an unwavering commitment to inclusivity, has not only reshaped the landscape of technology but has also illuminated pathways for countless young girls of color. Kimberly Bryant didn't just step into the technology sector; she kicked the door open and invited the next generation to walk through it with confidence and optimism.

Kimberly Bryant's story begins in her childhood in Memphis, Tennessee. Growing up in an economically modest household, the challenges she faced were numerous. Yet, her interest in science and technology was evident from a young age. She pursued an electrical engineering degree at Vanderbilt University, one of the few African American women in her program. This educational foundation, though rigorous and occasionally isolating, prepared Bryant for the hurdles she would later encounter and overcome in the professional world.

After graduating, Bryant worked in the biotechnology and pharmaceutical industries, including roles at companies like Genentech, Novartis, and Merck. She gained a wealth of experience; however, she couldn't ignore the lack of diversity in her field. Time and again, she found herself in spaces where she was one of the few, if not the only, women of color. This recurring experience planted the seed for what would eventually grow into Black Girls CODE.

In 2011, motivated by her daughter's experience at a tech summer camp where she was one of the only African American students, Bryant took action. She founded Black Girls CODE with a clear, ambitious mission: to introduce programming and technology to a new generation of coders from underrepresented communities. What started as a humble initiative in the Bay Area quickly expanded into a nationwide movement. Black Girls CODE offered workshops, hackathons, and after-school programs, creating safe, inclusive spaces where young girls could explore their interests in STEM without feeling out of place.

The impact of Black Girls CODE is undeniable. Since its inception, the organization has reached thousands of girls across the United

States and even expanded internationally. Thanks to Bryant's vision, these young coders are not only learning technical skills but are also gaining confidence and discovering role models in fields they once felt were inaccessible. Projects and events led by Black Girls CODE are often characterized by a sense of community and empowerment, encouraging participants to envision themselves as future leaders in tech.

Kimberly Bryant's advocacy extends beyond the technical training provided by Black Girls CODE. She is a vocal advocate for diversity and inclusion across the tech industry, frequently speaking at conferences, engaging with tech companies, and championing policies that support educational equity. Her thought leadership and dedication have earned her numerous accolades, including recognition as a Champion of Change by the White House and an inclusion in numerous influential lists celebrating impactful women in technology.

It's not just the technical skills that make Bryant's work so powerful; it's the holistic approach to mentoring that sets Black Girls CODE apart. By bringing in female engineers and technologists who share similar backgrounds and experiences, Bryant ensures that the program offers relatable role models to the participants. This creates a nurturing environment where ambition is not just encouraged but expected.

The ripple effect of Bryant's work manifests in myriad ways. Girls who participate in Black Girls CODE often go on to pursue advanced degrees in STEM fields, found tech startups, and become mentors themselves. Each success story adds to a growing network of women of color in technology, building a stronger, more diverse, and more innovative tech industry. This multiplier effect reinforces Bryant's vision and amplifies the program's impact far beyond its immediate participants.

However, the journey has not been without its challenges. Building and scaling an organization like Black Girls CODE demanded not just vision but persistence in the face of systemic barriers. Funding, recruitment, and community outreach required relentless effort and creativity. Bryant and her team have had to navigate a landscape frequently resistant to change, advocating tirelessly for the resources and recognition necessary to sustain and grow their work.

Despite these challenges, Bryant's resolve remains firm. She often remarks that her work is more than a career; it's a calling. This sense of purpose infuses every aspect of Black Girls CODE, from the curriculum design to the community engagement strategies. The result is an organization that is not only thriving but is also continuously evolving to meet the needs of its participants and adapt to the ever-changing tech landscape.

Kimberly Bryant's influence reaches the broader societal narrative about who can belong in tech. By spotlighting the capabilities and achievements of Black girls, she combats the stereotypes and biases that have long sidelined women of color in STEM fields. Her work serves as a compelling reminder that innovation thrives on diversity and that the potential for greatness exists in every community.

Looking towards the future, Bryant envisions a world where Black Girls CODE isn't necessary because diversity in tech is the norm rather than the exception. She dreams of an industry where every girl can see someone who looks like her in a leadership position, driving innovation and leading companies. Until that vision is realized, she remains committed to expanding Black Girls CODE, reaching more girls, and bridging the gap between talent and opportunity.

Kimberly Bryant's legacy will be defined not just by the organization she founded but by the countless lives she has touched and transformed. Her work stands as a testament to the power of inclusion, the importance of representation, and the limitless potential that is unlocked when barriers are dismantled. Through Black Girls CODE, Bryant is not only changing the face of tech; she is shaping the future, one line of code at a time.

Reshma Saujani: Coding for All with Girls Who Code

In the rapidly evolving landscape of technology, voices advocating for inclusion have been crucial. Among the most prominent is Reshma Saujani, who founded Girls Who Code in 2012. Her work has tirelessly aimed to bridge the gender gap in technology by empowering young women to embark on coding careers.

Reshma's journey didn't start in the tech world but in the realm of public service and advocacy. After running for a congressional seat in a historic race, she shifted her focus to a critical issue that persisted throughout her campaign—women's underrepresentation in technology. This pivotal moment set the stage for what would become a transformative movement.

Girls Who Code began with a simple yet revolutionary idea: Teach girls to code and inspire them to pursue careers in technology. The initiative took flight with just 20 girls in a borrowed classroom in New York City but rapidly expanded, resonating with a growing awareness of the pressing need for diversity in tech.

Through various innovative programs, Girls Who Code aims to equip young women with computer science skills. Camps, clubs, and immersion programs have been fundamental in reaching a wide demographic. By fostering a supportive community, the organization focuses not only on technical skills but also on confidence-building and leadership.

What separates Girls Who Code from other coding initiatives is its holistic approach. The program does more than teach coding languages and algorithms; it challenges societal norms and breaks down stereotypes that often discourage girls from pursuing STEM careers. Through mentoring, networking, and exposure to role models, Girls

Who Code helps students envision a future where they are at the forefront of technological innovation.

Reshma's vision is steeped in the belief that the tech industry should reflect the diversity of its users. To her, it's not just about coding; it's about creating a world where women have the same opportunities as men, where innovation is driven by diverse perspectives, and where girls feel they belong in the tech world.

The impact of Girls Who Code is evident in its alumni network. Graduates of the program have gone on to study computer science at top universities, intern at leading tech companies, and even start their own tech projects. By offering a launchpad, Reshma has enabled a generation of young women to break barriers and attain heights that seemed previously unreachable.

Reshma's efforts extend beyond the classroom. She's an outspoken advocate for policy changes that support her mission. Her Ted Talk titled "Teach Girls Bravery, Not Perfection" has garnered millions of views, propelling her message to a global audience. Through books, public speaking, and media appearances, she continues to push for systemic change and greater representation of women in tech.

The unique angle Reshma brings to the table is an unflinching focus on bravery. She emphasizes that girls should be encouraged to take risks, to fail, and to learn from those failures. This perspective marks a departure from traditional educational paradigms, which often reward perfection over audacity. Reshma's narrative shifts the focus towards resilience and courage, essential traits in the ever-evolving tech industry.

It's not just the tech skills that matter but the mindset. Girls Who Code instills a sense of purpose and ambition, encouraging young women to envision themselves not merely as participants but as leaders in technology. This empowerment often transcends the realm of coding, impacting other facets of their lives and future careers.

Corporate partnerships have played a significant role in scaling Girls Who Code. Companies like Google, Microsoft, and Facebook have supported the program, realizing that cultivating talent from diverse backgrounds isn't just good ethics but good business. These partnerships provide critical resources, mentors, and opportunities for the girls, anchoring the program's long-term sustainability.

Moreover, Reshma's advocacy extends to addressing gaps in technology access and education, particularly among underrepresented communities. By establishing a pipeline for girls from diverse backgrounds, Girls Who Code aims to democratize access to opportunities previously confined to privileged sectors of society. This inclusivity is at the very heart of the organization's ethos.

The broader impact of Reshma Saujani's work is twofold. First, it directly combats the gender disparity in tech, aiming for more women in technical roles. Second, it challenges societal perceptions and biases, gradually changing the narrative around women and technology. By showing that girls can be coders, engineers, and tech leaders, Girls Who Code shifts the cultural landscape one success story at a time.

The world Reshma envisions is one where coding is as accessible and normal for girls as it is for boys; a world where tech innovation benefits from a diversity of thought and experiences; a world where there's equal opportunity regardless of gender. Girls Who Code is making this vision a reality, one girl, one line of code, and one breakthrough at a time.

Reshma Saujani's unwavering dedication has not just inspired a movement but created a tangible pathway for young women to follow. She often shares stories of girls who've overcome immense odds to join the tech ranks, illustrating the real-world impact of her efforts. These stories serve as powerful reminders of what's possible when barriers are dismantled and dreams are given the support to become reality.

As we stand on the precipice of significant technological advancements, the work of Reshma and Girls Who Code becomes even more crucial. The tech industry is at a crossroads, needing to decide between perpetuating the status quo or embracing the change that diversity brings. In this landscape, Girls Who Code acts as both a beacon and a catalyst for a more inclusive future.

Reshma's journey with Girls Who Code is far from over. As the tech world continues to evolve, so too does her mission. New challenges will arise, but so will new opportunities to further the cause of inclusion. With each cohort of girls who graduate from the program, the tech industry inches closer to the equitable future that Reshma tirelessly advocates for.

In closing, Reshma Saujani's work with Girls Who Code is not just about teaching girls to code. It's about rewriting the narrative of who belongs in tech. By empowering a generation of girls to embrace coding, Reshma is planting the seeds for a future where innovation and inclusivity go hand in hand. Her story is a testament to the power of vision, resilience, and the unshakeable belief that every girl has the potential to change the world through technology.

CHAPTER 12:
FUTURE VISIONARIES

As we look to the future of technology, visionaries like Ruchi Sanghvi and Anousheh Ansari serve as beacons of innovation and inspiration. Ruchi Sanghvi, the first female engineer at Facebook, engineered the News Feed, fundamentally changing how we consume information and connect with each other. Her work underscores the profound impact one can have in the realm of social media and technology. Meanwhile, Anousheh Ansari, the first female private space explorer, has epitomized bravery and curiosity, inspiring countless individuals to dream beyond Earth's atmosphere. These women not only embody the spirit of pioneering but also remind us that the future of tech is limitless and inclusive. By breaking traditional boundaries and venturing into uncharted territories, they pave the way for the next generation of female engineers, scientists, and dreamers, demonstrating that no goal is too audacious, no frontier too distant.

Ruchi Sanghvi: Powering Facebook's News Feed

When you think of Facebook, one of the first features that comes to mind is its News Feed—a personalized, algorithm-driven stream of updates that transformed how people consumed and interacted with social media. The person who played a pivotal role in bringing this revolutionary feature to life was Ruchi Sanghvi.

Born in Pune, India, Sanghvi ventured into the tech world armed with a degree in Electrical Computer Engineering from Carnegie Mellon University. Her early career saw her tackle significant challenges at Oracle, but it wasn't until she joined Facebook in 2005 that her true impact would be felt. She was Facebook's first female engineer—an achievement that came with its own set of challenges and opportunities.

What struck Mark Zuckerberg and his team about Sanghvi wasn't just her technical acumen; it was her keen understanding of user experience. As she started working on Facebook's unique communication ecosystem, it became clear that she was a visionary. Sanghvi and her colleagues were initially tasked with refining Facebook's walls and profiles, but something much bigger was brewing.

The idea for the News Feed was initially met with a mixture of enthusiasm and skepticism. Sanghvi's team envisioned a dynamic stream of real-time activities from friends, which would eliminate the need for users to individually visit each profile. It was a revolutionary concept, but it posed complex engineering challenges, not to mention the potential ramifications on user privacy.

Ruchi Sanghvi broke down these challenges methodically. She knew that for the News Feed to succeed, it had to be intuitive and beneficial to the user experience. Sanghvi's approach was user-centric, ensuring that the feature would be both informative and unobtrusive. She and her team deployed advanced algorithms to sift through a user's contacts and select the most relevant updates to display.

On September 5, 2006, Facebook launched the News Feed. Despite meticulous planning, the feature was met with a fierce backlash. Many users were uncomfortable with the heightened visibility of their activities. Sanghvi, alongside her team, didn't just weather the storm—they actively listened and responded. They introduced privacy settings, giving users more control over what appeared in their News Feeds, thus reinforcing trust while maintaining the feature's core value.

This episode was more than just a test of Sanghvi's technical skills; it showcased her ability to navigate the complex interplay between technology, ethics, and human behavior. It didn't take long for the News Feed to win users over—its capacity to keep people connected and engaged was unparalleled. Today, it remains a cornerstone of not only Facebook but also the broader social media landscape, affirming Sanghvi's innovative foresight.

Her journey at Facebook was far from smooth sailing. As the first female engineer, she faced gender biases and challenges in an environment predominantly male. But if anything, these obstacles galvanized her spirit. She became a role model for many, emphasizing performance and skill over stereotypes. Her efforts helped lay a foundation for more inclusive practices in tech companies worldwide.

In 2010, Sanghvi left Facebook to co-found Cove, a company focusing on collaboration software, later acquired by Dropbox in 2012. This move marked another chapter in her career, proving her versatility and entrepreneurial spirit. At Dropbox, she served as the vice president for operations, helping scale the company during a period of significant growth.

Sanghvi's contributions have extended beyond her immediate roles. She's been an influential advocate for women in technology. Through her speaking engagements and mentorship programs, she has inspired countless women to pursue engineering and entrepreneurship, challenging the gender norms that have long plagued the industry.

Ruchi Sanghvi's story is a powerful testament to what can be achieved when technical prowess is paired with empathy and ethical consideration. Her efforts have not only changed how we interact on social platforms but also paved the way for future innovators to think critically about the human element in technology.

The legacy of the News Feed is not just in its functionality but in its philosophy. It's about creating meaningful connections in an increasingly digital world. Sanghvi's work reminds us that behind every line of code is the potential to make a profound impact on human lives, a lesson future visionaries can take to heart.

For aspiring female engineers and tech enthusiasts, Sanghvi's journey is an inspiring narrative of breaking barriers and making impactful contributions. In an industry that often resists inclusivity, her story serves as a beacon, demonstrating that vision, resilience, and empathy are as crucial as technical skill.

In a world where technology is often accused of creating distance and distrust, Ruchi Sanghvi's contributions stand as a counter-narrative—one that amplifies the potential of tech to bring us closer together. Her work has undoubtedly shaped the digital age and continues to inspire the next generation of tech leaders.

This is just the beginning. The path she paved beckons future innovators to embrace both the challenges and the wondrous possibilities that lie ahead.

Anousheh Ansari: Inspiring Space Exploration

Anousheh Ansari's name resonates with inspiration and ambition, especially among tech enthusiasts, aspiring female engineers, feminists, and those enthralled by real-life stories of determination. Her journey to becoming the first female private space explorer and the first astronaut of Iranian descent is nothing short of extraordinary. What sets Anousheh apart is not just her accomplishment of traveling to space but also her relentless pursuit of dreams against all odds, shining a light on the infinite possibilities of human potential.

Born in Mashhad, Iran, in 1966, Ansari's early years were defined by a fervent interest in the stars. Despite the societal constraints that often impede women's progress in scientific fields, her childhood dreams of space exploration remained undeterred. Moving to the United States with her family in 1984, she swiftly adapted to a new culture and language while excelling in her studies. Her academic journey culminated in a degree in electrical engineering and computer science from George Mason University, followed by a master's degree from George Washington University.

In 1993, Anousheh, her husband Hamid, and his brother Amir co-founded Telecom Technologies Inc. (TTI). This telecom start-up flourished under her leadership, eventually merging with Sonus Networks, a major name in the industry. The business success provided the financial stability and means to pursue her lifelong dream of space travel, but it was her perseverance and unwavering focus that propelled her to new heights.

Space represented more than a physical journey for Anousheh. It stood as the ultimate frontier, a vast expanse where she could contribute to humanity's understanding and serve as a role model for millions of women and girls worldwide. In 2006, after rigorous preparation and training, she made history by boarding the International Space Station (ISS) as part of the Soyuz TMA-9 mission. Her journey was not only a personal triumph but also a significant leap in the inclusion of private citizens in space exploration.

Ansari's influence extends beyond her journey to space. She is a vocal advocate for STEM education and empowering young women to engage in these fields. Through her work with the XPRIZE Foundation, she has outlined a vision for the future that involves tackling grand challenges through innovation and competition. The Ansari XPRIZE, a competition encouraging the development of private spaceflight, led to a renaissance in space travel and heralded a new era of commercial space exploration.

Anousheh's voyage aboard the ISS, lasting approximately nine days, was filled with moments of awe and scientific contribution. She engaged in various scientific experiments and relayed her experiences through an online blog. The transparency and accessibility of her journey captivated people worldwide, breaking down the often-unapproachable nature of space missions.

Her blog posts, written from space, conveyed a deep sense of connection with Earth, a reminder of our planet's fragility and the unity of the human race. These reflections fostered a broader dialogue on the importance of environmental stewardship and international collaboration in the field of space exploration.

The path Anousheh carved out is paved with her belief in the power of dreams and hard work. Her story underscores the idea that no dream is too big if one is willing to work tirelessly for it. The challenges she faced, from language barriers to the demanding physical and mental preparations for space travel, exemplify her resilience and unyielding spirit. Through her endeavors, she has championed the idea that exploration is not limited to astronauts from governmental space agencies but is a pursuit that can include civilians who dare to dream big.

Beyond her accomplishments, Anousheh Ansari has dedicated much of her life to philanthropy. Her efforts focus on creating opportunities for underrepresented groups in STEM fields. The initiatives she supports aim to dismantle barriers and provide equitable access to education and resources, fostering a more inclusive and diverse future tech ecosystem.

In conversations and interviews, Anousheh often speaks about the importance of curiosity, passion, and perseverance. Her message is clear: anyone, regardless of background or circumstances, can achieve extraordinary feats. She emphasizes the importance of nurturing a sense of wonder and encourages the next generation to pursue their interests vigorously and fearlessly.

Her story is not just a narrative of a single extraordinary individual; it is a clarion call to all who aspire to push the boundaries of what is possible. Whether in the realm of space exploration or any other field, the principles she embodies—passion, innovation, and commitment to making a difference—serve as a beacon for future visionaries.

Anousheh Ansari's journey continues to inspire because it echoes the limitless potential of dreams combined with determination. She has shown that the sky is not the limit; rather, it is just the beginning of new and uncharted adventures. Her contributions to space exploration, technology, and society exemplify the extraordinary impact one person can have when they dare to reach for the stars.

CONCLUSION

As we draw this inspiring journey to a close, it is clear that the landscape of technology would be incomplete without the remarkable contributions of pioneering women. Each chapter has unveiled stories of bravery, brilliance, and relentless determination. From Ada Lovelace laying the groundwork for modern computing to Anousheh Ansari pushing the boundaries of space exploration, the ingenuity of these women is vast and varied.

Consider, for a moment, the transformation of our world without their input. Without Grace Hopper's visionary work, we might be navigating a very different technological terrain. Imagine the absence of Evelyn Boyd Granville's role in space race triumphs or Barbara Liskov's pivotal ideas that underpin today's programming languages. Their stories remind us that innovation often blooms in the face of adversity.

The narrative of these trailblazers isn't just about their technological feats. More importantly, it's about breaking barriers – gender, racial, and societal. These women have rewritten the rules and broadened the definition of who can be a tech innovator. Kimberly Bryant and Reshma Saujani, for instance, are not only advancing technology but also democratizing it, ensuring that future generations have the opportunities that many of their predecessors did not.

Let's also acknowledge the emotional and psychological resilience required to challenge entrenched norms. Frances Allen and Radia Perlman, among others, had to constantly demonstrate their worth in a male-dominated industry. Their perseverance is a testament to their character and offers a powerful lesson: success in tech isn't just about intelligence; it's about resilience, courage, and the ability to envision a future that others can't yet see.

As technology evolves rapidly, the need for diverse perspectives becomes even more urgent. Fei-Fei Li's and Cynthia Breazeal's work in artificial intelligence and robotics shows us the importance of empathy and ethical considerations. In a world increasingly driven by algorithms, these visionary women remind us that human insights remain invaluable.

Furthermore, the entrepreneurial spirit showcased by icons like Susan Kare and Meg Whitman has set an incredible example for aspiring tech entrepreneurs. They show that successful leadership and innovation come from combining technical acumen with creativity and business savvy. Their adventures in charting new territories within massive organizations signal to every aspiring entrepreneur that the ceiling is indeed breakable.

In reviewing these stories, it's evident that the path forward is not a solitary journey but a collective one. Each breakthrough builds on the successes and struggles of the past, creating a stronger and more inclusive foundation for future generations. The contributions of women in technology aren't just milestones; they are stepping stones for what's next.

To every young girl coding her first line, every woman breaking into a tech career, and every reader inspired by these stories: know that you are part of a legacy. Your aspirations are valid, your contributions necessary, and your potential limitless. The giants on whose shoulders you stand were once in your position – armed only with a vision and the resolve to see it through.

Let's carry forward the torch passed down by these exceptional women and illuminate the future of technology together. The work is far from done, and the next Ada Lovelace, Grace Hopper, or Kimberly Bryant could very well be reading these words. Let this be your call to action, your motivation to push boundaries, and your reminder that you belong in tech.

This book, in closing, is more than a collection of biographies. It's a testament to the power of dreaming big and persevering against the odds. It's an enduring reminder that technology, in all its ever-changing glory, rests on the shoulders of those daring enough to innovate and bold enough to defy the status quo. Here's to the women who have shaped our past and to those who will undoubtedly forge our future.

The journey ahead is as limitless as the potential within each of us. Let's go forth and continue to revolutionize the world, one line of code, one innovative idea, and one empowered individual at a time.

Appendix A: Appendix

This Appendix is dedicated to supplementary information and additional resources that may enhance your understanding and appreciation of the trailblazing women we've highlighted throughout this book. Our aim is to provide context, expand on key themes, and direct you to other valuable tools and references that could empower you on your own personal and professional journey.

Further Reading

- *Hidden Figures* by Margot Lee Shetterly - A rich narrative that dives deep into the lives of the three African-American women mathematicians who played pivotal roles at NASA.

- *Lean In* by Sheryl Sandberg - Offers insights and guidance for women on leadership and success in the tech industry and beyond.

- *Code: The Hidden Language of Computer Hardware and Software* by Charles Petzold - An excellent primer on the foundations of programming and the evolution of computer science.

Online Learning Resources

Given the dynamic nature of technology and engineering fields, continuous learning is essential. Here are some valuable online platforms:

- **Coursera** - Offers courses taught by industry experts and top university professors. Check out the computer science and engineering tracks.

- **edX** - Provides access to courses from some of the world's best institutions. Perfect for deep dives into specialized topics.

- **Codecademy** - A hands-on platform for learning to code interactively, ideal for beginners.

Networking and Support Groups

Joining support groups and professional networks can be transformative. Consider these organizations dedicated to empowering women in tech:

- **Anita Borg Institute (ABI)** - Aims to connect, inspire, and guide women in computing and organizations that view technology innovation as a strategic imperative.

- **Women Who Code** - A global community that provides training, supports career growth, and connects women with mentorship opportunities in the tech industry.

- **Girls Who Code** - Focused on equipping young women with computing skills to close the gender gap in technology.

Inspirational Talks and Media

Sometimes, hearing stories firsthand can light a spark. Here are some recommended talks and documentaries:

- **TED Talks** - Seek out TED Talks by women in technology, covering a range of topics from breaking barriers to innovative future visions.

- **Code: Debugging the Gender Gap** - A documentary that exposes the dearth of American female and minority software engineers and explores what is being done to address the gap.

- **STEMinist Podcast** - A show that highlights the stories of women in science, technology, engineering, and mathematics.

Events and Conferences

Attending conferences can be a great opportunity to learn, network, and get inspired. Consider these renowned events:

- **Grace Hopper Celebration** - The world's largest gathering of women technologists, named in honor of Grace Hopper.

- **Women In Technology Summit (WITS)** - Offers a variety of sessions designed to foster skills development, innovation, and leadership.

- **Tech Up For Women** - A hub of information that allows women to stay current on technology advancements, risks, and solutions.

Acknowledgements

Many have contributed to the making of this book. Our heartfelt thanks go out to the individuals interviewed, their families, researchers, and historians who provided invaluable insights and anecdotes. Your stories are the heartbeat of this work.

We hope this Appendix serves as a useful guide, encouraging you to explore further and to keep pushing the boundaries—just like the exemplary women we've honored in these pages.

www.ingramcontent.com/pod-product-compliance
Lightning Source LLC
Chambersburg PA
CBHW051256050326
40689CB00007B/1218